Perfect Parenting & Other Myths

Frank Main, Ed.D.

CompCare Publishers   2415 Annapolis Lane   Minneapolis, Minnesota 55441

Main, Frank 1944-
    Perfect parenting & other myths.

    Bibliography: p.
    Includes index
    1. Parenting—United States.   2. Child rearing—
United States.   3. Child psychology.   I. Title.
II. Title: Perfect parenting and other myths.
HQ755.8.M35   1986   649'.1   86-2295
ISBN 0-89638-093-9

Cover design by Susan Rinek
Index by Audrey DeLaMartre

    Inquiries, orders, and catalog requests should be addressed to
    CompCare Publishers
    2415 Annapolis Lane
    Minneapolis, Minnesota 55441
    Call toll free 800/328-3330
    (Minnesota residents 559-4800)

            3   4   5   6

                88   89   90

CONTENTS

PREFACE

One of the most intimate things one can write about is parenting. As I started to unravel the parenting techniques I believe in, I realized I was unraveling my strongest sentiments about love, God, and my country. In that process, it's difficult to say exactly when my views about parenting solidified; they probably haven't.

In any event, to prevent this preface from becoming an autobiography I think it's fair to say of myself, and perhaps others, that I began learning about being a parent as a child. Later during the Viet Nam war I learned about cooperation and leadership. Paradoxically, my teachers were my troops—the lesson stuck. Leadership isn't commanded or awarded by virtue of title—parent or lieutenant—it's won. For this I am grateful to Larry Fitzpatrick, Harvey Franklin, and others like them. I hope they are alive and well somewhere, rearing their children.

Shortly after the war I finished my graduate education and was lucky enough to have a teacher who gave me the time and questions I needed to find reason in the world again—to be encouraged. To Tom Edgar I owe much, not just for the information he generated, but for what he taught me about teaching—about professing.

At about this same time Mary and I were becoming parents. Without any play on words intended, if it weren't for her none of this would have been possible. At those moments when I've felt most inadequate and most self-centered, Mary always managed to rekindle my social interest. And without question, our daughters, Katie and Buffie, have been my ultimate source of encouragement. They don't aspire to be like me, but I aspire to be like them.

Over the years I have had the help and encouragement of many Adlerian colleagues and friends. In particular, Dr. Ray Corsini, who for no reason at all other than the fact that I was presumptuous enough to ask, read a sample of this manuscript and provided a wonderfully blunt and encouraging critique. I thank him for giving weight to the phrase, "the opportunity to overcome adversity."

On the subject of courage, I'm indebted to John Nield, whose creativity and courage in confronting his own mortality have been a source of encouragement to others and provided anecdotes for this book.

The grist for this book, the cute and dramatic stories, wouldn't have happened were it not for the Family Counseling Center at the University of South Dakota. Also, without the support of my colleague and friend Gordon Poling, the center would never have survived during its early years. His encouragement and flexibility gave me gumption—important stuff, gumption.

As I've engaged families over the years, there has always been a fine line between earnestness and humor. In most cases I've managed, with the good will of these families, to be encouraging without being condescending. To say that communicating this process has been difficult is an understatement. Were it not for the encouraging eye of Bonnie Hesse, the editor of this work, the task would never have been accomplished. She has been my editor, friend, and most importantly, as a mother of three sons, teacher.

In addition, there are several friends who by virtue of their willingness to critique my work, have served as sounding boards: Nancy Zuercher and Craig Volk. And, to my prairie friends Ann and Roger Smith a special thanks; to Ann for the hours of drawing done in an effort to depict the anecdotes recorded here, the drawings will find their audience another day; and to Roger, father of three daughters, for his unabashedly earthy evaluation of my work.

To my secretary Corine Jurgensen, a note of thanks for her willingness to help at the drop of a hat. In addition, she has provided a mirror for me to see what it was like working with an only child.

Most importantly, I am indebted to the hundreds of families that must remain anonymous, the families who *are* this book, those who shared their imperfections and joys for our benefit. Without their courage, support, and *gemeinschaftsgefuehl* over the years, this book would be absent of its humor and substance. The experiences these families have shared include desperate as well as garden-variety concerns, the concerns we all have. And finally, to my students I owe a special debt. Through their queries, hard work, and criticism, the Family Counseling Center has flourished.

For the most part, "our" parenting problems are the concerns of all parents. And since we must look for explanations for our predicaments within our families, this book is for all of us.

To my family: my daughters, Kate and Buffie,
and my wife, Mary.

PART ONE
THE PERFECT PARENT MYTH

1
PARENTING IN THE EIGHTIES

Super(parent)...that Perfect Person against whom we compare ourselves in order to fully experience failure.

—Ellen Goodman
Close to Home

THE PERFECT PARENT MYTH

On the set of "The Brady Bunch" the doorbell rings. Mr. and Mrs. Brady rise together and walk arm in arm to see who's there. A pretty sight, right? Now the scene changes to bedtime. The Bradys sit upright against the headboard carefully groomed in ironed pajamas, smooth bedcovers. Enter Marcia, Bobby or another one of the kids who sits on the end of the bed, making polite conversation. A lovely vision— great kids and perfect parents!

Have you ever met people who live like this? Of course not! The Mother or Father of the Year is a myth, plain and simple, perpetrated by advertisers of detergent, box cakes, floor wax, a variety of TV situation comedies, and, of course, our kids. Kids would like parents to believe that these phantom figures—the perfect parents—reside in the homes of their best friends. After all, "Susie's Mom and Dad let her go to the concert," so Susie gets to go when they don't.

Other parents also contribute to the illusion by acting as if some-where, somehow parents can transcend the basic nature of the human condition and achieve perfection—like on "The Waltons." Referring to what he calls the "legend of the Waltons," sociologist Ashley Montagu writes that Americans place excessive demands on the family "in the form of myths and misconceptions which, in fantasy but not in fact, have converted the home into a shrine and the family into a band of angels."

As a society, we link our basic parental dignity to our ability to get rid of ring around the collar and static cling. That's because we're supposed to be in control of everything. As anthropologist Margaret Mackenzie notes, "We are a culture nearly addicted to individual control." Psychologists add to the notion by suggesting that if we follow prescription x or y, our children will be under our control. But just as it's ridiculous to attach our parental dignity to media hypes, it's also ridiculous to assume we can parent perfectly if we follow certain steps. What recipe for behavior can control a three-year-old during a two-hour concert?

Parents as a group are seduced by the culturally ingrained value to be the "best"—to compete, to win! We are coerced, prodded, and told we can—if we try harder—be Number One, the best, perfect. So, most of us get caught up in the competitive cultural fantasy that we can parent flawlessly if we get whiter wash and adhere to the new parenting "system" the neighbors are using.

This cultural fascination with flawless and effortless child-rearing has created a mythical parent who has become the fictitious yardstick by which all of us measure ourselves. *We discourage our children and ourselves by pursuing the fantasy!*

Think about the impossibility of the assumption for a minute—if a person is perfect there is no more room for improvement! That's an impossible goal. Part of the problem is a genuine lack of understanding—adults in general (parents in particular) think they can control things they can't. But more about that later. For now, it's enough to know that there is simply no such thing as perfect parenting. And for a lot of good reasons, there shouldn't be. There, you're off the hook!

This book is a celebration of imperfection. Most of us have worried about our hair-twisting, nail-biting, obnoxious kids. Those who haven't are exceptional members of an elusive minority who should be sharing the bliss with the rest of us. We all have common concerns, imperfections, and intermittent bouts of joy and success with our spouses and children. In that, there ought to be a message—we all share the human condition and ought to enjoy the humor it provides. Little can come of striving for fictional goals, especially if we stake our reputation on the behavior of a pre-schooler whose major ambition in life seems to be to stake his reputation on ruining ours.

Have the courage to be imperfect! Celebrate your fallibility! There is room for improvement—there always will be!

ME-STURBATION

Without tracing the whole of human creation, it is a matter of historic reality that human beings have always been social animals. As a species they were without talons, claws, wings, feet, or a large muscle mass, so in order to hunt, eat, and overcome natural adversaries, humans had to join with others. In fact, most of their efforts to overcome their inferior position on the planet required cooperation with others.

History itself is a record of human socialization. Since survival against the elements required group action, *belonging* became a necessity. When herds of human beings began to think in terms of survival of the species and the community, they made the transition from herd to society. Individuals and/or families developed self-consciousness and a concern for others, thus laying the cornerstones of civilization.

In contrast, when people cease to hold these values in common, the fabric of a culture is undermined. For this reason, during the last two decades we have come dangerously close to a return of the herd.

The psychologies of the sixties and seventies, which professed "doing your own thing," "pulling your own strings," dropping out, finding one's center, mantra, or guru have paradoxically jeopardized families and society. For twenty years the mentality of "me-sturbation" has promoted the illusion of self as center—another lovely fiction.

Unfortunately, the shrinking planet leaves few personal oases and mountain top retreats. According to Alfred Adler, the late Austrian psychiatrist, our existence is bound by an "iron-clad communal logic" which intensifies with each generation of nuclear arms. Like it or not, we reside on a planet whose limits become more finite with each generation, and if we allow ourselves to think it, our universe probably has similar limits. Thus, we are by necessity social animals, and in order to survive we must belong, and to belong we must cooperate—not drop out, or dominate.

The question now is, How do we bring these ideas to life within a society? Historic evidence and hope for the future seem to have come full circle and now rest upon the family. From the self-centeredness of the earlier decades we have come to a renewed understanding of the importance of the family and an enlightened view of the parent's role.

A youngster's first social experience (the first sense of belonging) is with parents and siblings. When we think about all that's at stake in these early family experiences, the responsibility is awesome. Parents must model and teach their children responsibility, cooperation, and a sense of community.

WE INSTEAD OF ME

Today most parents overlook the importance of belonging. However, Adler used clear, though perhaps outdated, language to highlight it. He believed that our primary need was to belong, to be accepted for our uniqueness, to acquire a sense of competence, to acquire a sense of esteem, to feel meaningful, to feel significant—to acquire what he labeled "felt plus."

Adler's concept communicates well a fundamental principle—that we need to feel like we belong! We need to feel a part of a greater whole in a cooperative way, while still feeling independent and autonomous. Most of what we do as adults is designed to produce these feelings. If we aren't able to belong, we can be discouraged to the point of depression and neurosis. Discouragement for an adult is devastating, but for a child discouragement, or not belonging, is entombment.

Discouraged children become depressed, mischievous, lazy, or vicious, and grow to be adults who are more so. *The question we ask is: "Who discourages them?" Wrong question. Instead we need to ask: "How does a child become discouraged and at what price?"* Most of us know what it's like to be passed over for a promotion or told we're not fast enough, smart enough, or aggressive enough for the job. We don't take it well, and we may spend hours daydreaming about professional and social opportunities for revenge. We usually revel in thoughts like, "If I could get that turkey in my department just once," or "On the racquetball court I'd show 'em."

Now think about the equivalent situation for a child—let's say a five-year-old. First, he or she must look up at the looming adult authority figure—a view of groins and armpits. That's discouraging! As if

4

the size differential weren't enough, this towering giant asks unanswerable questions such as, "Why are you so slow?" "How could you forget what I told you?" "Why did you break that?" The implications are clear even to the youngest children—they're incompetent. That's very discouraging!

Based upon a litany of inadequacies, children begin to feel that they don't matter; that they aren't capable of making a contribution; that they don't *belong*. Once children feel discouraged, it's difficult for them to muster the courage necessary to try to belong by being responsible: by contributing, helping, sharing, and cooperating. In most cases kids will be discouraged and resort to irresponsible attempts to belong. Discouraged children decide, without being aware of it, that they will belong at any price—even if it means being the best at being the worst.

HOW DID WE GET HERE?

Parenting in the eighties has brought some special problems which, although sobering, carry a silver lining. For one thing, our children probably have more freedom because of the rise in democracy itself. For another thing, from the time youngsters are old enough to turn a channel they hear the messages of television, like "kids are people too!" As a result, even at very early ages children believe they are entitled to dignity and respect. Imagine that! And that's just the beginning! They also believe they are entitled to independence, money—and power. However, the part our children missed—the part that they weren't taught—is that along with all those benefits goes responsible cooperation. *"Who didn't teach them?" "Who's to blame?" Wrong question! No one's to blame! The right question is: "How was responsibility lost?"*

How have kids become so powerful and, at the same time, irresponsible? In earlier times a youngster's responsibilities in the home were not only mandatory but important. If the child forgot to milk the cow, several significant things happened. The family went without milk! Secondly, the cow's milk might dry up and a source of revenue might be permanently lost. Furthermore, the family and the community as a whole believed that God himself might intervene to discipline the child, further highlighting the negligence. There were real consequences—

hardships—imposed on the family which clarified the meaning and reinforced the significance of irresponsibility.

Today, things are different. Society in general is more affluent. The world of work has been redefined and even the word *work* has a different meaning. Hardship is having to unload the dishwasher! Extraordinary inconvenience is having the microwave in for repair. Oppression is discovering our budgets won't allow us to drive more than 50,000 miles a year. If Junior is asked to walk home from school, he considers it an adventure and calls the weather service for conditions; and, if a disaster should strike and the home video recorder goes on the blink, panic sets in. We are a people with great material wealth. *Yet, affluence in itself is not offensive, but the irresponsibility it can create is.*

As technology has developed, families have found it more difficult to find things that matter for kids to do. Sixty years ago if Billy didn't chop wood for the fire the house was cold. If Billy didn't do his chores, it mattered! Today if Billy forgets to start dinner while Mom is at work, the family can eat at McDonald's—it really doesn't matter. So today a parent's task is to insure that family matters matter. You see, these situational problems created by technology have caused parents to lose sight of a fundamental principle—children must contribute to the survival of the family in ways that really count. Why is that such a crucial dynamic? Because everyone must have a meaningful role in family survival in order to foster belonging, independence, and responsibility.

Many systems of psychology were developed in order to cope with the rise in democracy. The "Me decades" spawned psychologies which had the individual as center focus, but at the expense of the group. In general, the different theories have gone to both ends of the spectrum, liberal and conservative, and back again. Extremes always have well-intended philosophical assumptions, and even biblical "proof" on occasion, to establish their credibility.

Extending the application of these psychologies to parenting styles, the thinking polarized at the extremes of dictator and directionless parent, both of which are at odds with the goal of raising responsible children. For instance, both positions ignore the need to live life with, and often for, other people. Furthermore, neither position presents a workable approach to parenting because neither teaches children the responsibility necessary to keep pace with their rights.

6

PAMPERING GARDENERS VS. PUNITIVE GATEKEEPERS

Why don't these approaches work? Let's look at characterizations of the extremes for insight. The first group of impassioned parents, the liberal, Spockian, laissez-faire parents, championed their cause and felt just as righteous as their "opponents," but had a useless assumption—that tender loving care (T.L.C.) was the necessary and sufficient condition for parenting. The human cultivators simply provided a liberal dose of T.L.C. and allowed the child to blossom. These parents were pampering gardeners.

The second group of impassioned parents represents a nostalgic return to conservative parenting dogma with principles based upon "might makes right." Disciples of this doctrine are punitive gatekeepers who dare parents to discipline punitively. The gatekeepers would have parents believe that there is a biblical admonition which canonizes controlling the lives of their children even with force when necessary, i.e., "spare the rod and spoil the child." Unfortunately, these strategies only provide the illusion of control. And, they frequently initiate pathological loss of control. The advocates of one extreme—the gatekeepers—cite religious conviction as their justification for action, while the others—pampering gardeners—rally around the laissez-faire legacy of Rousseau.

How did we get to extremes, anyway? Has it been just the simple progression of people trying extremely hard to do an extremely good job? So what's wrong with that? Well, it sounds okay, doesn't it? Just like the slogan of the candidate for President some years back—"Extremism in the defense of liberty is no vice." It sounded good at first, but on second thought there were pitfalls. The candidate meant well, but the campaign slogan didn't work. Parenting extremes don't work either.

What choice then do parents have? By now, the answer is probably obvious. There is no safety, no guarantee in any one solution. That's what the extremes really are, attempts to guarantee. There is no rule book nor any such thing as perfection—there is "only" doing the best you can, coupled with understanding the value of encouragement, using common sense, cultivating your child's sense of belonging, believing in the innate goodness of the child, trusting in the child's innate abilities, and using disciplinary measures that have logical consequences.

All of us have good days and bad. All of us make mistakes and do silly things from time to time. But the task of being an encouraging parent—not a perfect parent—is possible. And taking the common sense approach, with the above concepts in mind, there are advantages for both you and your children. Before you commit yourself to this common sense system, let's see what *parenting with encouragement* means.

Encouraging parents are probably different in one simple respect. They have become or learned to be realistic about how much they control their kids. They don't rush to claim credit for accomplishments which are the child's nor do they assume responsibility for the child's irresponsibility. They are leaders instead of commanders; they're believers instead of nay-sayers. This simple shift in attitude usually results in critically different behavior—both for parents and children.

ARE YOU READY FOR THIS?

Is parenting with encouragement a workable approach for you? Check the following signposts to see if you're headed in the right direction.

1. Natural Consequences

All of us have experienced the rushed, harried, or finicky morning eater who doesn't eat a decent breakfast. If you're one who checks the post office "ten most wanted list" for your name every time your second grader leaves the house without breakfast, you're not ready to try natural consequences. But, if you recognize that your child has the eating habits and storage capacity of a camel, you're ready to allow the natural consequence (hunger) to take effect. (The suggestions for natural consequences in chapter 6 will help you take advantage of nature's educators.)

2. Effective Communication

You overhear your kids playing house—they're using your "sermonettes" as dialogue. If you think it's cute, preach on. But if the replay has a nasty ring, you're ready to listen rather than preach.

(The effective communication skills in chapter 5 will help you listen to your kids, and, paradoxically, they may hear you for the first time in years.)

3. Encouragement as a Technique

If you still draw sympathetic listeners at parties when you talk about the turmoil imposed by trying to please your hyperactive child, suffer on. But if your whining empties the room, suffering may have outlived its usefulness for you and you're prepared to allow the child to "handle" it, whatever "it" is. This attitude—"you can handle it"—is encouraging. As Dr. Rudolph Dreikurs phrased it, "Never do for children what they can do for themselves." If you believe that parents ought to be guides and not stretcher bearers, then you're ready to use the suggestions in chapter 5.

4. Logical Consequences

All of our kids have indicted us with the infamous, "Oh yuk, not that again." Our knee-jerk response is to make restitution by cooking a better meal. Another is to force feed the child, regardless of how s/he feels about certain food. "Oh yuk" isn't just a rejection of our menu: it's a rejection of our very being and threatens our image as "good" parents.

But pursuing our self-esteem through the stomachs of others is useless. If you have the courage to find your esteem through your own efforts and not someone else's digestive system, you're ready to try logical consequences. "I am sorry you don't care for it. You are welcome to fix yourself a PBJ (peanut butter and jelly sandwich) if you clean up after yourself, or you may excuse yourself." A logical consequence is no more than a natural consequence extended to include the realities of nature, hunger, and the reality of the "family order," your right to be a person and not a short-order cook. Logical consequences, as defined in chapter 6, take others and the family order into consideration, offer choices, and are instructional as well as disciplinary.

5. Understanding Birth Order

If you have often been puzzled by the disproportionate amount of time your middle child devotes to fairness, ask yourself how many baby pictures the child has. "No baby pictures" becomes the symbolic cry of middle children. They were often squeezed out of the picture. The impact of being squeezed makes their keen eye for injustice much more understandable and their view easier to handle. Similar insights, offered in chapter 3, for the oldest, youngest and only child will make their behavior more comprehensible.

6. Parents as People

A final test of your readiness for this book is dependent upon the priority you place upon your marital intimacy. If you have sweaty palms, chest pains, and lapse into a coma when you think about your kids leaving home and your oldest is six, you're not ready for these principles. But if you have sexual fantasies about the good old days and envision a rekindling of the old flame and sex in front of the fireplace, you're ready!

THE IMPERFECT PARENT—A GUIDE FOR MORTALS

The chapters to come offer diagnostic, disciplinary, motivational, and communication techniques for situations which typically occur in family settings. Also, general guidelines are provided so you can transfer the principles from ordinary situations to misbehaviors your children haven't even thought of yet.

To be effective, parents have to understand children's behavior. Parents have a propensity for asking the wrong diagnostic questions of themselves and of their kids.

Parents ask *"Who's at fault or to blame?" Wrong question! The right questions are, "What emotional purpose does this behavior serve? How do kids feel they belong by doing these things? And, how do we (parents) contribute to the problem?"*

2
THE POWER AND PURPOSE
OF CHILDREN'S BEHAVIOR

Children need encouragement like a plant needs water.

—Rudolf Dreikurs

PURPOSE OF EMOTIONS

According to Adler, all behavior is purposeful and designed to provide a general sense of "belonging." If that's the case, what purpose is served by children's sloppy, lazy, or belligerent behavior? Offhand, the purpose would seem to be antisocial and antithetical—it is totally useless, fosters rejection, and undermines belonging. But if adults look closely, they will discover that underlying the behaviors are emotional goals which are sought by children and paid off by adults. Dr. Rudolph Dreikurs described four categories of childhood misbehavior, which he called "mistaken goals":

1. Attention-getting mechanisms
2. Bids for power
3. Acts of revenge
4. Assumed disabilities

You might ask, as many parents have, "How are these goals mistaken? They sound pretty accurate to me." But, *"How are these mistaken?" is the wrong question. The right question is, "Why do children select uncooperative vs. cooperative behavior?"*

From the child's view the answer is pretty simple—children think these misbehaviors will satisfy their emotional goal to belong. They're half right. For example, the child thinks, "I belong if Mother is busy with me," and proceeds to interrupt Mom repeatedly while she's on the phone. Mom provides plenty of attention, but it's all negative: "I *told* you not to bother me while I'm on the phone! Go to your room!" So paradoxically, the belonging sought by the child is lost. The rejection, discouragement and confusion, which are obvious to the child, begin to have a cyclic discouraging effect.

If children fail to acquire belonging through socially useful, cooperative, contributing actions, they settle for belonging at any price—belonging by being the best at being the worst. Discouraged children misbehave (either by attempts to get attention, power, revenge, or by assuming disability), because they have lost the courage to find their place by doing the useful thing. Unfortunately, they choose a useless behavior—that is, children do things which they think will achieve their goal (getting attention, for example)—which does get attention but does not achieve their emotional objective of belonging.

Similarly, once children realize that power will give them leverage over other family members, they seek power as an attempt to gain belonging. For example, children learn quickly that hunger strikes can have a powerful and controlling effect on the family—"You can't make me eat that...." Over the short term the child feels, as do the parents, like s/he has "won." Indeed, parents can't force the child to eat. Because the child's power is acquired through obstinance and stubbornness, the child is often emotionally or physically rejected instead of validated and loses any sense of belonging. S/he feels in control—but alone. Thus, the useless goal of power wins the skirmish (not eating) but loses the objective, the need to belong.

Why, you may wonder, do children think like that? Probably because they are *discouraged*, that is, they have lost the courage to find their place by doing the useful thing. *Discouraged* means literally to lose one's courage. And children are easily stripped of their courage, especially by their parents. Let's say the child feels particularly in need of a reassuring hug. The child who feels encouraged can ask for what s/he needs. That's useful. The discouraged child who needs a hug kicks his brother in the shin to get Mom's attention. That's useless.

To illustrate the devastating impact discouragement has on children, consider the following examples. Compare the useful with the useless bid for attention, for instance. Note how subtly but dramatically discouragement can catapult children into one of the four "useless" goals.

Example 1—Attention

Encouraged child: "Mom, I need a hug."
Encouraging parent: "Come here, dear. These's nothing more important than a hug."

Encouraged child: "Mom, I need a hug."
Discouraging parent: "Don't give me that—you're stalling for time so you won't have to do your homework."
Discouraged child, now seeking attention: "I'm hungry. I have to have a snack first."

Example 2—Power

Encouraged child: "Dad, I moved the woodpile around back today. Did you see it?"
Encouraging parent: "Yeah, looks good. Thanks. I wouldn't have gotten to it until fall."

Encouraged child: "Dad, I moved the woodpile around back today. Did you see it?"
Discouraging parent: "I'll say—why did you put it there? All the kindling is on the bottom and it'll be impossible to get."
Discouraged child, now struggling to regain the power he lost when stripped of his sense of contribution: "I knew you wouldn't be satisfied no matter where I put it so I just dumped it there. I'm not moving it again!"

Example 3—Revenge

Encouraged child: "Mom, I babysat for the Martins today on short notice, so I left without cleaning my room. I'll be babysitting for them every week now."
Encouraging parent: "I bet you feel good about that. You'll probably enjoy the extra money. And I'm sure you'll remember to take care of your room."

Encouraged child: "Mom, I babysat for the Martins..."
Discouraging parent: "Is that why you left without picking up your room? You're not going anywhere now! You have responsibilities here first, you know."
Discouraged child, now seeking revenge for being hurt: "Yeah, right! Next time I'll take all week to do my room and you can call the Martins and tell them I quit!"

Example 4—Assumed Disability

Encouraged child: "Dad, I'm not going to sports camp this summer. I'm no good at anything."
Encouraging parent: "I can tell you're discouraged, but I hate to see you being so hard on yourself."

Encouraged child: "Dad, I'm not going to..."
Discouraging parent: "Go ahead and quit! Then you'll really have problems—no one likes a quitter."
Discouraged child now retreats further from useful behavior with silent withdrawal.

Children become discouraged in one of two ways. First, when they make an effort or contribution, adults discourage them by failing to acknowledge or appreciate either. Second, adults often rob children of the opportunity to overcome adversity—we do for children what they could and should do for themselves. In that way, our parenting strategy pirates their responsibility.

For example, when the librarian calls to inform your youngest about overdue books, you might hunt up the books, return them, and pay the fine. By intercepting the child's opportunity to overcome mild adversity, you have sucked away his or her sense of competency. Every time an adult acts like a highwayman and robs the child of competence or courage by stripping away responsibility, discouragement will mount. Most often such actions by adults are compounded by comments like "Well, I returned your books for you and paid for your fines for you," clearly implying that gratitude is expected for a favor not requested.

As discouragement accumulates, children become increasingly irresponsible. Very likely, the next time the child in the example above has overdue books, s/he'll simply wait for Mom to return them! Then think of how the conversation might go: "I had to return your books *again*—you are really being irresponsible! No more TV for this week." Children's discouragement can be transient or long-term, depending on the extent to which parents ignore effort and contribution and strip children of opportunities to overcome adversity.

The disadvantages of discouragement can be fully appreciated if you consider the carry-over behaviors of the discouraged child who's learned to get attention at any price. Take the attention-seeking child, whining and screaming while you're the dinner guests of friends. The whining tyrant demands top billing and competes with your host for attention. It's embarrassing at best!

To take another example, a four-year-old who is allowed to pick out his/her own clothes develops independence and eventually, a sense of style. By comparison, when a parent not only picks out the wardrobe but dresses the child, the child's courage and dignity are siphoned away. Two messages are clear: 1) the child's choices are not as good as the parent's; and 2) the child can't overrule parent, and so becomes discouraged. S/he may ultimately refuse to dress himself!

Still another example of encouragement would be parents who allow their sixteen-year-olds to exercise their privilege of driving the family car as well as the opportunity to assume responsibility for their insurance coverage and operating expenses. By comparison, parents who give their young driver the car carte blanche, complete with gas card, steal responsibility and thereby discourage the child.

Discouraged, useless behaviors are on the useless side of life and employ competition, detraction, and selfishness. By comparison belonging, potency, competence and esteem are legitimate ends. According to psychologist Walter O'Connell, "All people need and get power." Everyone is entitled to positive potency, but when children, or adults, are discouraged about their prospects for useful/cooperative potency and belonging, they compensate by exclusively demanding potency through useless behaviors.

If parents understand that the child's underlying emotional goal is to belong, they can avoid the pitfalls of useless behavior. Parents usually overlook the fact that misbehaving children need misguided adults to pay them off in order to persist in their misbehavior. In order

15

to deal with useless behaviors, adults have to understand the purpose of emotions.

EMOTIONAL PEOPLE-MOVERS

Children's emotional goals are not that dissimilar from adult methods of interaction, and might be better understood if we reflect on a typical adult transaction. Consider for a moment the husband and wife who are arguing violently. During the battle the husband explodes in a fit of rage and smashes one of their his-and-her matching cups on the floor. Upon discovering that the broken cup is hers, the woman exclaims, "That was my cup!" The man's cool response—"Sure—you didn't think I would break mine, did you?"

This anecdote suggests that fits of rage aren't fits at all, but controlled outbursts designed for an emotional purpose—to move others! We call temper into service when the situation demands. Emotions have always had biological and psychological survival value, but many times children and adults engage in people-moving emotions in useless rather than useful ways.

In order to change misbehaving children, adults must recognize the child's "useless behavior" and avoid paying off the child's emotional demands. *The question adults usually ask when confronted with misbehavior is "Who's to blame?" Wrong question! The question ought to be, "How am I feeling and reacting to these misbehaviors?"* To be an encouraging parent you must take a different diagnostic tack—instead of watching the child, watch yourself! By recognizing your reactions, you can avoid paying off useless emotional goals; then your emotions can redirect your behavior, and subsequently the useless behavior of the child.

Let's explore for a moment the four categories of children's useless behaviors, adding the corresponding adult emotional reactions. The charts on the following pages demonstrate how children's need to belong serves as a motivating force; it is an all-consuming goal, pulling children, and adults for that matter, into action. Children seeking to belong at any cost will develop a "private logic" which supports their efforts, no matter how much this private logic contradicts common sense.

Private logic is no more than a person's private emotional conviction about events. If someone is discouraged, the private logic and subsequent behavior become increasingly selfish and useless. When that same person is encouraged, the private logic reflects more common sense (sense which takes others into account).

According to psychologist Dr. Raymond Corsini, children can be taught to pursue belonging through what he calls "the four R's." These four R's have been framed in the charts as useful, constructive goals of belonging. As you can note in figure 3, these goals include Respect, Responsibility, Responsiveness, and Resourcefulness.

Encouraged children ultimately accomplish their goal to belong. Discouraged children don't. In both cases the behavior pattern is cyclic. Discouragement stimulates useless behavior, absence of belonging, and more discouragement, while encouragement produces belonging, useful behavior, and more encouragement.

As children pursue belonging through the useless goals of misbehavior, emotions are intense. During these conflicts, adults' emotional reactions correspond directly to the four goals of children. In the following examples note how the children's behaviors produce predictable emotional responses on the part of the parents.

1. Attention-getting

When children demand attention and services, adults feel annoyed, frustrated, and fatigued.

- Your seven-year-old appears to be suffering from narcolepsy five days a week. Seven A.M. Saturday morning he miraculously recovers and doesn't miss a single cartoon.
- Your twelve-year-old daughter has an apparent visual perceptual disorder. She can neither find nor identify her own clothing with the exception of her baseball glove and cap.
- Your sixteen-year-old has the earliest case of arteriosclerosis on record and is unable to remember to put gas in the car.

Now ask yourself: are my kids aware of my feelings? Some parents have difficulty answering this. If you doubt it, think about the look on your twelve-year-old's face when you start to search for her baseball glove. Not only does she smile as you scurry around looking for her possessions, but she probably sits down to watch you work! At times

17

CHILD'S GOAL OF BELONGING:
Discouraged Child

USELESS BEHAVIOR		CHILD'S PRIVATE LOGIC
• **Attention-getting:** Whining, pest, nagging	▶	• I belong when others pay attention to me or serve me
• **Bids for Power:** Disobedience, rebellion, eating problems	▶	• I belong when I am the boss or when I can do what I want to do
• **Revenge:** Vandalism, stealing, bullying, lying	▶	• I belong when I can hurt others as much as I think I've been hurt
• **Assumed Disability:** Giving up, school drop-out, academic failure	▶	• I belong as long as I am not confronted with my inadequacies

Fig. 1

CHILD'S GOAL OF BELONGING:
Encouraged Child

USEFUL BEHAVIOR		CHILD'S PRIVATE LOGIC
• **Respect:** Considerate, caring and cared about	▶	• I belong when I get respect from those I respect
• **Responsibility:** Independence, decisiveness, dependability	▶	• I belong when I am responsible and am given the opportunity to be
• **Responsiveness:** Altruism, love, response to the needs of others	▶	• I belong when I can love and help others as much as I've been helped and loved
• **Resourcefulness:** Expression of talent, creativity and ingenuity	▶	• I belong when my talents are accepted, nourished, and developed

Fig. 2

ADULT'S EMOTIONAL RESPONSE TO CHILD'S BEHAVIOR

DISCOURAGED CHILD

USELESS BEHAVIOR	ADULT EMOTIONAL RESPONSE
Attention	Annoyed
Power	Angry — Defeated
Revenge	Hurt and Hurtful
Assumed Disability	Hopeless — At a loss

ENCOURAGED CHILD

USEFUL BEHAVIOR	ADULT EMOTIONAL RESPONSE
* Respect	Pleased and Respected
Responsibility	Proud and Happy
Responsiveness	Loving and Appreciative
Resourcefulness	Heartened and Secure

*The C4R System, Alternative Educational Systems, E. Ignas & R. Corsini (1982:210) Peacock Publishers, Inc., Itasca, Illinois 60143.

Fig. 3

CYCLES OF BEHAVIOR

CYCLE OF DISCOURAGED CHILD'S BEHAVIOR

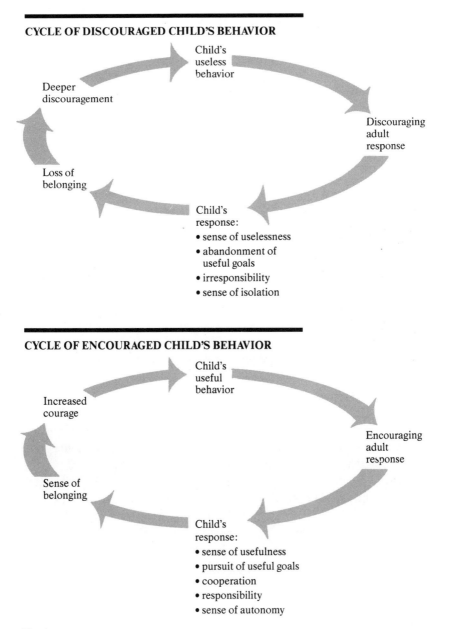

Child's
useless
behavior

Deeper
discouragement

Discouraging
adult
response

Loss of
belonging

Child's
response:
• sense of uselessness
• abandonment of
  useful goals
• irresponsibility
• sense of isolation

CYCLE OF ENCOURAGED CHILD'S BEHAVIOR

Child's
useful
behavior

Increased
courage

Encouraging
adult
response

Sense of
belonging

Child's
response:
• sense of usefulness
• pursuit of useful goals
• cooperation
• responsibility
• sense of autonomy

Fig. 4

like this there is no force on earth strong enough to camouflage your emotions. Kids know!

Then why in heaven's name do they continue to annoy you? In these episodes the explanation is simply attention. Children assume, below their awareness, that they have a place in the family only when they are receiving special service and attention from those around them. "If Mom doesn't find my clothes, she doesn't love me." "When Dad brings me gas for my car, I feel my status as royalty."

These episodes also clearly illustrate another downside of discouraged behavior: children have no motivation for independence or autonomy if adults assume responsibility for them.

Half-Hearted Attempts to Control "Little Pests"

Kids effectively "bug" us because our behavior, when we're annoyed, amounts to hollow, inconsequential gesturing—like shooing flies. We don't really act, we just pretend to act. Useless behaviors predictably produce reactions but they provide children with a distorted sense of belonging, and in the process place children in competition with everyone.

In order to be a "pest" the child must demand our attention when our attention is needed by someone else. Therefore, the child competes selfishly for attention against everyone else. Annoyance is the typical adult reaction to these episodes, not anger, hurt or desperation—just annoyance. Below our awareness we're saying, "Gosh, this kid keeps me busy" or "There they go again, I don't think I have the energy to handle it today." Our annoyance triggers shoo-fly behavior: inconsistent, repetitive, half-hearted actions that usually provide exactly what the child demands—attention.

For example, have you ever called someone on the phone and heard an obnoxious misbehaving child in the background disrupting the conversation? Have your own children targeted you for unmerciful pestering once you put that piece of plastic to your ear? Probably! Children seem to know, instinctively, that you're tethered to the wall by that plastic cord. They dart around the fringe of your tether with such speed that you suffer whiplash. You probably yell something like, "Can't you see that I'm on the phone?" They have just wrapped you around the wine rack and you're wondering if they know you're on the phone.

22

Their attention-getting antics range from demanding to talk to the banker who's calling you about overdrafts, to seizing control of the kitchen countertops. You might respond by trying to carry on the conversation as if nothing is happening, or by pleading and coercing a little. Finally, the caller empathetically rescues you from yourself. "Sounds like you need to hang up now." When you shoo flies, you divide your attention and effort unevenly between the caller, or someone else, while "pretending" to deal with your children. There's an absent-minded aspect to your behavior which betrays your intentions. Take heed! When you're feeling annoyed, that's your emotional warning light—your kids have you hypnotized. You're doing tricks for them and don't know it.

On the positive side, the adult's annoyance can be a great diagnostic tool. When parents are feeling annoyed, they know service is being sought by the child and they can choose to behave affirmatively instead of shooing flies. Diverted attention results in absent-minded service, attention, or both—doing for children what they could be doing for themselves.

Adults support attention-getting behavior because they believe, mistakenly, that to refuse to provide service is equivalent to being a bad parent. We delude ourselves into believing we are "good parents" until we discover our kids have auctioned off a week's stay at our house as a fund-raiser for the junior prom. Then reluctantly we wonder if we've done too much for them.

2. Bids for Power

When children make successful bids for power, adults feel defeated and angry.

- Your four-year-old son has refused to eat his peas and you have spoon fed him and sent him to bed. In the morning you discover one large mouthful of mushy peas compressed under his pillow.

- You have been meticulously toilet-training your three-year-old daughter and happen to be the guest of another family at a nice restaurant. The hostess seats you in a quiet corner booth, and your three-year-old announces her need to go "pooh pooh" and does.

- You tell your seventeen-year-old daughter to be home by midnight or she'll be grounded for the rest of the semester. She comes home at dawn and tells you that next week is finals week.

Seeing ourselves in these episodes, we may smile because they're not happening to us at the moment. When we live these episodes we feel defeated, angry, and even enraged. However, although the incidents are not funny, parents need to make a real effort to see the lighter side whenever they can. Humor is often the sanest and easiest way for parents to assume problem ownership.

Recently a very frustrated mother was explaining her evening ordeal to me. "First she wants a drink, then she wants the lights on, then off, then she needs to go to the bathroom, then she needs a story, then an aspirin..." "Who gets the drink?" I ask. "I do," she said. "Who gets the light?" "I do!" "Who gets the aspirin?" Finally, breaking out in laughter she said, "I'm really great at making her the boss, aren't I."

"But how do I get to humor from anger?" you ask. According to Walter O'Connell, we can't take life too seriously because no one gets out of it alive. Metaphorically, humor can be cultivated by recognizing the difference between what is controllable and what isn't; by accepting the fact that you can control your own emotions but not those of another. Then you have a chance of seeing the brighter side. But if you catastrophize, you will be immobilized by your own fear.

Looking at our behavior and rhetoric following an episode illuminates its absurdity. Chances are we are saying to ourselves, "Who's the boss here?" or "Who does she think she is? This is my house!" Our authority is threatened and we are feeling powerless. That's it—power! Kids, having grown accustomed to adult bids for power and control, are making an attempt to demonstrate their own power. Below their awareness lurks this notion: "When I make them do what I want or prove to them they can't make me, I am a force to be reckoned with in the family."

It's useless for adults or kids to seek belonging through power over others. Adults often initiate these struggles or respond to invitations they could ignore. Anyone who has tried to digest a child's food for him (or her) can attest to the futility of it all. Adults who have force fed or withheld food in order to control the diet of a child realize how absurd "personal power" is. Once parents truly experience their inability to control the life of another, they are a step closer to controlling their own lives. *It is a surprising, but accurate paradox—control is gained by giving it up!*

Attempting to belong by trying to control the behavior, attitude, or emotions of another is useless. Useless behavior of children is uncooperative, and by definition competitive. That is, children seek to belong at the expense of others. These attention-getting mechanisms, power plays and acts of revenge undermine and hurt others while making hollow motions toward the child's real goal of belonging. Useless behavior, whether it is used by adults or children, mistakenly applies our cultural value of competition to human relationships. While competition is a useful value in athletics, and perhaps business, it's inappropriate and destructive in interpersonal relationships. Thus, distinguishing between those circumstances that appropriately call for competition and those which require cooperation becomes the subtle measure of a good spouse, parent, and citizen.

We tend to label the child "bad" as a result of his/her behavior, but it's important to make a distinction between bad and useless. Essentially, children we label as "bad" are those who have not been educated: they haven't been taught when to compete and when to cooperate. Having labeled the behavior as bad, we generalize to include the child: now the child is "bad" as well. This daisy chain of generalization is discouraging and counter-productive. It's true the child's behavior is useless but we shouldn't conclude that the child is "bad." Therefore, if we try to think in terms of useful vs. useless instead of good vs. bad, we will afford children the dignity and worth they're entitled to and encourage them in the process. "Bad" strips dignity and worth, whereas "useless" doesn't imply anything but futility and wasted effort. Making this distinction between "bad" and "useless" may seem like a semantic exercise, but it makes a profound difference in a child's view.

If we think in terms of "useless" vs. "bad" we actively separate the deed and the doer. We're saying, "I dislike your actions but not you." Everyone is entitled to worth and dignity in the normal course of events. Yet, "respect" is not granted as a function of station or authority. Parents often try to perpetuate the fiction that respect is deserved simply because one is a parent—no unique feat actually.

We conveniently forget how incensed and rebellious we were (or are) in the face of autocratic models. We often perpetuate the fiction that we can kick our children in the pants, only to discover that our "child" is now 6'3", 235 pounds, and big enough to eat hay. Then we spend the last two years of the kid's high school career, white-knuckled and breathless, wondering how things got out of control. If adults pursue the useless goal of dictator, they will experience the same end as all despots, no matter how benevolent—dethronement. Similarly, children who try to model or defeat the powerful adults around them will gain fleeting power, but lose their sense of belonging indefinitely. A more realistic goal within the family and community must be to win, not to force, cooperation and to generate respect for those whose respect we seek.

3. Revenge and Counter-Hurt

When children seek revenge, adults get hurt and want to counter-hurt.

- You have bribed, chastised, and finally spanked your four-year-old son for messing his pants. Now he does it only when your bridge club meets or when you take him to preschool. Since he continues to make a mess of things, neither bridge nor pre-school is possible.

- You are a yeller and a good one. You have just finished blasting your eight-year-old son for the dismal condition of his room, his school performance, and his overall insensitivity as a human being. He appears to have heard none of it. In a final act of desperation, you spank him for whining. Three hours later you find he has lashed the family's dog to the backyard fence and is gleefully scourging the pet with your tennis racket. How could he do this?

- You are recognized as a pillar of the community, head of the school board, head of the church development committee, and president of the state Rotary Club. Your eldest daughter is a constant source of concern. Recently you have grounded her from all high school activities because she violated curfew, withheld her allowance because she has refused to do her chores, and called her best friend's mother forbidding the girls to associate with one another. During noon hour the following day she is caught shoplifting in the mall where your business is located. Embarrassment and humiliation permeate every pore of your body, and you can't understand why she did it!

The theme is the same in each of these incidents, although it may appear different. In every case the adult is saying below awareness, "Why does this kid want to hurt me?" The emotional response of most parents is hurt, counter-hurt,—a tendency to get even. This response by the parents is exactly what children ask for through these misbehaviors. Children who pursue revenge feel they "belong" only when they can hurt others as much as they've been hurt. From a parental perspective this is illogical, but it fits the child's private logic perfectly. Assessing a child's motives through adult eyeglasses is a mistake. If a parent spanks a ten-year-old, the child feels justified in hitting back, justified in hurting someone as much as s/he's been hurt. From the private perspective of the ten-year-old, the more people hurt via vengeful deeds the better s/he feels.

Hurt can also be generated through emotional as well as physical pain. For example, a parent once said to her offspring, "I don't expect much from you and nobody else does either. Frankly, I wonder why your friends continue to include you in their group—they're all doers and you're a watcher!" After a steady diet of this disparaging fare, the youth feels like striking back at adults in general through major mischief, vandalism, alcohol and substance abuse, and petty theft.

When the child's objective is revenge, the last thing a parent should do is generate counter-hurt. Employing punitive strategies with these children is akin to throwing gas on a fire. The net effect of punitive discipline is a roaring conflagration. Punishing vengeful kids only contributes to potential pathology.

A painful example of this can be found in our penitentiaries. Threatening inmates with "the hole" and solitary confinement has negligible or compounding effects on revenge-seekers. While working in the penitentiary I heard many inmates say of solitary confinement, "Ain't no big deal, I can do sixty days standing on my head." Ironically, punitively disciplined inmates were usually just a little tougher after their punishment than they were before. This is not to say that criminals shouldn't be locked up—they must be. However, rehabilitation through retribution is ineffective in most cases and nearly impossible under the best of conditions.

The uselessness of punitive counter-hurt strategies becomes obvious when taken to its ludicrous end. "If you hit me, I'll shoot you. If you shoot me, I'll bomb you. If you bomb me, I'll nuke you." Such wisdom seems to be the fodder of modern diplomacy.

Having served in the Marine Corps in Vietnam, I don't qualify as a pacifist, but I have learned that it's difficult for people to impose their version of "good" upon others without incalculable destruction.

If parents choose power and hurt as a means of control, they must expect sabotage and revolution. Authority isn't commanded, it's earned. The era of ruling with a big stick is long dead as every super powerful parent and nation must eventually discover.

When people are deeply hurt, their intuitive reaction is to get even. Revenge is not a very glamorous characteristic for an adult or child to own; nonetheless, it exists. If you saw the boy who lashed his pet to the fence fall off his new ten-speed bike, would you grin coyly and say beneath your breath, "It serves him right"? If you didn't, you are unusual, and if you did, you are like the rest of us who want to get even after being hurt.

The youngster whose parents have been punitive and unreasonable have set in motion strong feelings of revenge and counter-hurt. Below his/her awareness, the youngster is saying, "I am recognized and belong when I have the capacity to hurt others as much as I've been hurt." This is illogical, of course, but emotionally it is reasonable. Typically, revenge becomes a child's goal when adults have ignored or disregarded the child's dignity and worth. Autocratic approaches are never quite powerful enough to control the child. As children get older and more physically powerful, independent, and vengeful, it's harder for the adult to exert enough force, physical or emotional, to "control" the child—pain for that young person becomes a badge of courage.

4. Assumed Disability

When children assume a disability, adults feel hopelessness and despair.

- You have exhausted all possible resources in an effort to teach a nine-year-old boy simple addition, to no avail. No amount of punishment, or reward, seems to affect him. Math has long been a family value and everyone, including the dog, can count with ease. Yet, this kid has withstood punitive restrictions and forty-six pounds of M & M's, and his teacher tells you now he daydreams through math. You give up!

- Your five-year-old girl has a problem—she seems incapable of zipping her own coat. You have tried everything, but she seems to prefer being left alone to behave as an infant rather than make an effort. Quite accidentally, you witness her zipping a doll's dress requiring similar skills, and you have a nagging feeling you've been had!

- Your son slept through junior high and has just taken his achievement tests in high school. The results are miserable, and so is he. You threaten and finally offer him the bribe of a lifetime, his own car. The next day he drops out of school. Your bewilderment is matched only by your despair.

Adults react to this kind of behavior with a sense of hopelessness. What possibly could be gained from such useless, self-destructive behavior? The answer, although not visible to the naked eye, is simple and direct. Children reason, quite correctly, that if they are left alone and make no effort at all, their overwhelming inadequacies will not be publicly displayed time after time.

Why make an effort and flaunt before God and everyone else your miserable ineptitudes? It is far easier to refuse to make an effort and preserve some sense of dignity. Logically there are some apparent errors; it may not make sense, but emotionally it's a stroke of self-pre-serving genius. Dreikurs called this type of protective behavior an "assumed disability," meaning that if children are able to convince others that they are truly incapable, they inevitably are relieved of most of life's responsibilities. Not a bad ploy, all things considered.

So, to get the child back on the useful track, look for the hidden agenda. *The wrong question is: "How can I move my child to action?" The right question is: "Why does my child feel it necessary to assume disability?"* Now comes the adult's emotional response which plays a pivotal role. If the adult hangs in there and doesn't give up—for example, waits until the child does zip her coat—then the child can't relinquish responsibility. In order for the assumed disability to work, kids have to get parents to throw in the towel. The corrective message to adults is, "Fight the feeling." Parents who succumb to hopelessness discourage themselves and the child. "Okay, I'll zip you up since you're such a baby."

The role of emotions is clear in each of these episodes. The general purpose of emotions, that is, to move people, is witnessed specifically in all four goals. Yet, there are particular emotional goals of kids that are especially troublesome to each of us. Which of your children is most like you emotionally? Would that child also be the one that causes you the greatest difficulty? Think about it! Probably the child who is most like you is the child who is capable of anticipating your moods and emotional games and uses them better than you do. Upon close inspection you will often discover that your problem child is a mirror of your own emotions! That is a sobering prospect.

If kids are mirrors of our own emotions, and if we expect them to change their behavior, we will have to change ours. If you're still reading, you're beginning to recognize that there really are no rose gardens or panaceas in this book. There is no chapter entitled "The Easy Way." Cooperative relationships take time and work to develop, but the end result is always worth the effort made. Like a healthy thirty-year marriage, parenting with encouragement is supported by equal distribution of labor, responsibility, and affection. Like marriage, this kind of parenting requires work, and the payoff is trusting, courageous, responsible children and useful behavior.

This chapter demonstrated the purpose of behavior and illustrated the emotional payoffs our kids seek and how we inadvertently provide those payoffs. Actually, this is enough to know in order to parent sensibly, but it may also be helpful to understand why discouraging, useless behaviors develop. Although adults are responsible for encouragement and discouragement, that is by no means the entire story. Discouragement also has origins in sibling relationships and, most importantly, in the child's own creative view of these relationships.

The next chapter will explore the effects of sibling relationships on the behavioral style of the child and the family.

3
NO BABY PICTURES:
The Family Constellation

Everything can be something else as well.
                                    —Alfred Adler

BIRTH ORDER: FACT AND FICTION

Recently "the birth-order factor" has experienced a trendy revival. The order of your birth explains your fate, so the theory goes. If you are the firstborn, you'll be a hard-driving Type A personality, destined to become a company president or a commanding general. If you're the middle child, you'll be the emotional squeaky wheel, making a career out of righting injustice. And if you're the baby of the family, you're bound to be fun-loving, lucky, and spoiled.

Birth order isn't a fatalistic alternative to phrenology, astrology, or tea leaf telepathy. As Alfred Adler, the pioneer in birth-order research, aptly pointed out, "Everything can be something else as well." Our position in the family is predictive, but not fatalistic; yet it does have psychological impact. We don't control the order of our birth, but all of us are uniquely influenced by our biological lot. It follows, then, that interpretation of a child's birth order can provide insight into his or her emotional style.

As if their position in the family weren't enough, most kids between the ages of two and eleven, as mentioned earlier, see a world of "groins and armpits." But within this generally one-up (you), one-down (them) world, children develop their own individual view of the situation. And they act—or better yet, "act up" accordingly. Their behavior is simply their means of moving and manipulating others—creative ways of finding their place through the use of powerful emotions—and these creative patterns are always useful and useless to varying degrees.

To summarize, on the one hand there are attributes developing out of each birth-order position which contribute to the child's belonging and emotional survival. On the other hand there are sources of discouragement—"groins and armpits," which are the springboards for useless emotional goals and behavior. Ultimately, as parents we must seek ways of derailing misbehavior or discouragement and ways of encouraging the uniqueness of each child.

NO BABY PICTURES AND OTHER PERILS
OF FAMILY BIRTH ORDER

Some years ago, while conducting a workshop for a group of teachers, I asked a group of middles what it was like growing up as a middle child. After a poignant pause one group member responded sarcastically, "...No baby pictures!" The group burst into recognition laughter, followed by a brief but intense chorus: "Right on!" While the spokesperson didn't capture the uniqueness of each member, he did reflect the kindred spirit of middles.

In group settings I urge people, grouped by birth order, to plan a party and record their festivities on a large piece of newsprint provided. The results are usually educational and always fun. Each birth-order position—oldest, middle, youngest and only—gives potential for certain emotional styles, within which we will find our own uniqueness as well as that of our kids. Let's look at the parties planned by the various birth-order groups to see the typical strengths and weaknesses of each.

Over-Organized Oldests

What's it like being an oldest child? The party planned by the oldest is indeed planned. Make no mistake about it, firstborns will have a well-organized, successful party with much attention to detail. There will be superb delegation of chores with ample supervision. Oldests strive to be successful. Typically, firstborns turn their party-planning process into competition—competition for the best, the first done, the most efficient. This punctilious, task-oriented style produces results.

Oldests are achievers. (The first fifteen of the first seventeen astronauts were firstborns or firstborn males!) Their party is totally reliable and responsibly done. It's always a proper affair—very proper.

Although it's well organized, the party smacks of ho-humness. Let's face it, it's boring! A case in point: one group of oldests decided upon a "seed exchange" (as in Burpee's best new tomatoes and carrots) for their entertainment. Depending upon your point of view, a seed exchange is either fascinating or very boring—trading tulip bulbs, carrot seeds, and cucumbers. Even in their play, firstborns get organized. It is the over-organization of the oldests' style that can be discouraging.

Sources of Discouragement for Firstborns

Like it or not, oldest children have a propensity for excess. They are generally too task-oriented, bossy, serious, rigid, and right. What oldests don't take on themselves, "we" (adults) supply for them via expectations, demands, and parenting responsibilities. The price paid for these excesses can include anxiety about achievement and perennial struggles for power with bosses, spouses, and kids.

For those of us who are not number one, it's difficult to understand how those who are could be discouraged. At times we catch glimpses of the stuffy inflexibility, but we fail to empathize with the burdens of the firstborn. Although being number one provides an aura of royalty, it is a working monarchy. There is no question the throne provides power, but with it come the troubles of the kingdom. The responsibilities never end and the burden continues even during sleep. Oldests literally have nightmares about failure. To fail is to lose one's crown and the power that goes with it. Obviously, the anxiety and pressure can be overwhelming.

Firstborns are prone to demand perfection of themselves. If this need to achieve took place in isolation from everything else, it might be palatable, but it always requires that one's performance be compared to everyone else's. The striving in itself isn't useless—it's the requirement that everyone else be rank ordered to determine one's level of perfection that's useless!

Firstborns often feel martyred and overworked without recognizing that their suffering isn't due to others' insensitivity or unappreciativeness, but to their own inability to say no! "No" is a foreign expression in their vocabulary which only occurs when they critique the performance of others. Eldests can be terribly successful and terribly anxious, driven and neurotic. This imperative of success can support neurosis.

Encouragement Strategies

Derailing useless misbehavior amounts to relieving the oldest child's periodic sense of discouragement. In a word—encouragement. Later in chapter 5, these techniques will be presented in detail, but the following could be considered a shorthand formula for encouraging oldests. Since oldests will press their own noses to the grindstone, you probably won't have to. Lighten up! Try to avoid evaluation and comparisons. Firstborns are likely to spend far too much time rating themselves in relationship to others as it is. Minimize, as much as possible, competition between siblings. Don't compare their grades, athletic, or artistic talent to their brothers and sisters. And, perhaps most importantly, don't ask your oldest child to assume your parental responsibilities no matter how trivial or convenient.

Strong-Willed Secondborns

Since seconds aren't always middles, let's talk first about secondborns who are last! First and second kids are as different as night and day. In fact, firstborn kids of different families are more alike than first- and secondborn kids of the same family. Since the oldest has nailed down his/her areas of success, the second will choose different ways to succeed. There are exceptions, of course. For example, if first and second children are more than four years apart and of the opposite sex, they are likely to be like only children or two oldests. There are differences between second and middle children as well. Middles are often pressed by the trailing youngest; seconds never are.

Secondborns view the world from the perspective of Avis. They try harder but are always second best. They are forever catching up. They must be told by others, even at age thirty-five, that they are successes in their own right because they themselves don't realize it. Second children have perseverance and strength of purpose.

Parties generated by second children look like the assembly directions for a new bicycle, mechanical and incomplete. The group questions the purpose of the exercise, reflecting their independence, autonomy, and reluctance to meet the expectations of others. They think planning a party is silly. Recently, when I asked to see the party of the secondborns, they looked at me devilishly and said, "We didn't do it!" They just didn't do the exercise. On one hand their emotional self-assurance is a relief to parents; in many ways they seem much more self-actualized than their older siblings. Yet, their independence and perseverance can mushroom into stubbornness and include a very self-destructive edge. These self-destructive tendencies often go unrecognized and result in vicious self-defeating behavior.

Sources of Discouragement for Second Children

The second child may have the distinction of being second and youngest, or second and middle. While both have benefits, they also have discouraging elements. The second child, who is truly second and never experiences the presence of a younger sibling, develops tremendous compensatory strivings which can lead to an extremely competitive style. Consumed by striving to overcome, seconds can self-destruct in their own competitiveness. To ride the bike of life like their older siblings, they may mount it at the top of a hill and ride tenaciously down at breakneck speed, knowing that the only thing to stop them is the brick wall at the bottom. Or, secondborns decide to evacuate altogether the arena established by the oldests and try their luck in a completely different place. (However, the secondborn's choice is literally out of the sight and mind of the firstborn.) The sense of never getting one's just reward generates feelings of exaggerated independence or competition.

Encouragement Strategies for Secondborns

The parenting message is obvious. Do not highlight competition between siblings! First and second children will pit themselves against one another without your help. If parents escalate the problems by adding offhand comments like "Why can't you work a little harder and get the grades your brother does?" the intensity of the struggle

35

will result in the rebellion of one or both kids. Avoid, as much as humanly possible, providing a source of opposition against which a second child can rebel. If the first and second children are close in age, look for opportunities to provide the second child with responsibility and authority. Finally, appreciate the second child's strengths for what they are. When you are prone to chide these children for stubbornness, reframe the description and show appreciation for their "independence." When you are prone to chide them about competitive behavior, express appreciation for their "perseverance."

Middles: Masters of Fairness

Middle children are truly unique; some say outright strange, but why wouldn't they be? For years they have been overshadowed and out-performed by the oldest and out-charmed by the youngest. And, as if it weren't enough to be squeezed into oblivion by one's siblings, Mom and Dad highlight these inequities through a conspicuous absence of baby pictures. It comes as no surprise that middle children tend to weigh life on the scales of justice.

A party by middle children is described in emotional terms and looks dramatically different from the party of the oldests. This one is not organized. Each group member of the party planners is given "air time" and the ideas and feelings are added to the party as they go along; what is produced looks like an emotional collage! The party also reflects their feelings of injustice. Because they haven't been heard, recognized, or attended to, middle children plan activities which require intimacy and interaction. Self-disclosure and "getting to know you" games are often included.

The group decision-making process often consumes most of the time available for planning. As a group they are intent on giving everyone an opportunity to be heard. Consequently, they often are consumed by their attempts to gain consensus or count the vote.

Sources of Discouragement for Middles

It is easy to guess the "problem" child in the family of three boys or three girls. It's the squeaky wheel in the middle. If adjacent siblings

36

are of a different sex, the patterns may vary from the typical. However, it is often the squeezed middle who presents problems.

Middle children can smell injustice even if it's hermetically sealed with good intentions! In one party-planning exercise a group of middles planned to play "Texas golf," a game in which four people share the best ball hit by a foursome, thus giving everyone the best possible score—a fair shot at long last.

Middle children make good contract negotiators. You'll find middles gifted with the ability to pick apart the opponent's proposal; they're also the ones who mediate the differences among members of a negotiation team. They know immediately what they're against, but have difficulty deciding what they're for. They are not to be depreciated for this, because they have come to learn, through practice, primarily that which they oppose.

As adults, however, middles don't experience extremes in behavior which plague the rest of us. Fewer middles abuse substances, commit violent crimes, or become mentally ill in proportion to the other birth-order positions. Middles tend to be "copers." Over the years they have developed great coping skills, and although they may be a bit neurotic and a pain in the neck, they survive.

Encouragement Strategies for Middle Children

If parents could imagine how it feels to be squeezed literally out of the picture, they would find it easier to encourage middle children who often appear rebellious and negative. Rather than complaining about the middle children's whining about fairness, a suggestion for parents is to do the unexpected and credit them for their sensitivity to others. Make a place for them in the family routine and utilize democratic techniques for distributing responsibilities. Don't use middles as your emotional buffer or thermometer for the family. Do your own emotional bidding and when middles take on injustices for one family member or another, credit them for their effort, but never assign them such responsibilities.

A case in point is reflected in the family that was blessed with an academically gifted middle and an athletically gifted oldest. The athlete was on the verge of failing biology when the parents intervened by bringing the middle into service to tutor the eldest. Although the academic outcome was positive, the oldest child knew the special relationship and agreement that existed between the middle child and Mom and Dad. Humor helped to soften the impact of the middle child's alliance with the parents, but the arrangement might have created a temporary imbalance between the parents and all the kids.

It's crucial to recognize that each child must have a place in the family through positive contributions, attributes, and uniqueness. While the child must belong, s/he must belong through a sense of personal potency or autonomy. These two notions, the sense of autonomy and of belonging, are not opposites, but merely two points on an emotional line. Parents must learn to recognize the effort made by the middle child and be sure the child receives visible recognition. This doesn't mean the parent must reward and pay the youngster for effort.

The next time your kids are embroiled in a squabble and ask or coerce you into intervening, decline. "I'm sorry you're not getting along, but you can handle it." Don't try to balance the scales of injustice. Declare yourself unwilling to do so and withdraw from any attempts on their part to incorporate you into such activity. Recognize and pronounce to the world that "life is unfair," and you have gone out of the justice business! You can't single-handedly insure fairness! But you *can* save yourself a great deal of anguish if you recognize that assuming responsibility for your children's problems strips them of the opportunity to overcome adversity.

Creative and Competitive Youngests

The youngest child is truly the crown prince or princess. This child, by some fluke of fate, is cute, charming, charismatic, and helpless. Initially it's a puzzle, but closer observation reveals a lifestyle which, from the outset, was considered one of royalty. Youngest children don't expect to do anything; others have always done for them. As royalty, youngests expect more of life emotionally and materially. Recently I voiced these observations in a group and there were strenuous objections by a thirty-two-year-old youngest. I conceded it may have been different for him and prepared to move on. Suddenly he began to smile and I couldn't help but ask why. It just occurred to him that he stopped messing his pants at the age three because his older sister paid him to. He had considered quitting earlier, but until that time there didn't seem to be anything in it for him. It had suddenly dawned on him that his style was self-serving and materialistic, but charming as could be.

The youngests' party is always fun. Unlike the parties of the oldests, youngests are creative enough to avoid boredom. The "little kids" are spontaneous and want party hats, costumes, decorations, live music, and "prizes." Youngests always include plenty of creature comforts. Their parties include the finest amenities: food, sauna baths, and hot tubs—in short, pleasures of the flesh. Just because they're thirty-five doesn't mean they can't have fun.

One particularly memorable bash involved a Hawaiian luau complete with pig roast on location in Maui. Not surprisingly, this fantasy was the work of a group of youngest school teachers employed in a small remote community in the western panhandle of Nebraska. Youngests never let practicality and reality interfere with creativity and spontaneity. Of course, some things may be overlooked: who is going to bring food? provide entertainment? do the decorating? clean up and— pay for it? If pushed for details, they'll say the party will be catered.

Sources of Discouragement for Youngests

For siblings looking down on the youngests, it's difficult to understand how they could be discouraged; after all, "they had everything." It's difficult to deny. Mom and Dad's earning power usually increased greatly between the birth of the first and last child, so it was much easier to be generous, easy-going, and overly solicitous. Youngests, like the oldests, have status as nobility, but there's a big difference. The youngests have all the privileges without any of the *responsibilities*. That sounds wonderful at first, but closer observation reveals people who may have no accomplishments to call their own. Others always do for them.

To be served as nobility may mean the development of "no ability." Youngests often feel indecisive in major decision-making situations; if a big decision must be made, they call someone who knows. Consequently, at thirty-five, the youngest's professional accomplishments may be referred to as "dumb luck" by older siblings and parents. If they were lucky, that must mean they weren't competent. Unfortunately, youngests often accept this assessment of their ability. Never having practiced decision-making, responsibility, organization, and independence, youngests may not be very good in these areas. The emotional by-product is a nagging feeling of inadequacy.

As adults, this inadequacy can reach epidemic proportions. It's not unusual to see the youngest child in counseling, suffering from an overdose of dependency. These dependencies include reliance upon spouses for approval and acceptance, dependence upon the boss for direction, guidance and reward, and dependence upon one's children for a sense of esteem and belonging. In normal doses we all require some of this, but when the approval of others becomes all-consuming we feel like the puck in an air hockey game. Total dependence upon anything or anyone is discouraging. It is only exceeded in its gravity by total independence.

Encouragement Strategies for Youngests

You may wonder what you can do to avoid dilemmas for the youngest children. Simply this: *Never do for children what they can do for themselves!* That may be the best advice provided for raising any child. There are obvious nuances to this simple edict, but the message is clear. We cannot expect our children to become instantaneously independent, responsible, and caring at the age of eighteen, if they haven't had an opportunity to practice these behaviors all along.

Children cannot be expected to act responsibly if they have never been given responsibility.

Youngest children in particular are often stripped of opportunities to do for themselves. Often as not they have two or more mothers—older siblings—to serve them. Multiple Moms contribute to the despair by denying youngests an opportunity to fail, succeed, and contribute.

Occasionally there are dramatic exceptions: youngest children who are emotionally and professionally independent. In these cases the youngest child is usually four or more years younger than the next oldest sibling. Although the person may be chronologically the youngest, s/he is like an only child psychologically.

For the youngests, parents must train themselves and the children to balance belonging and independence. And further, parents need to recognize, value, and redirect the youngest's creativity. Years ago a client described wild fantasies to one therapist after another. Each therapist in his turn pronounced the fantasies "abnormal" and prescribed his own brand of exotic therapy. Finally, this whimsical soul found his way to a therapist who quickly suggested the client write stories about these marvelous fantasies. Ian Fleming did exactly that, and rest is literary history.

Onlys: Hardy Hybrids

Onlys, as you might guess, are hybrids. Like most hybrids, they are easily spotted. Contrary to stereotypes, they are not tender-limbed nor weak-rooted. The opposite is true. Only children usually achieve and produce, but most hybrids have their quirks and only children are no different.

The parties planned by only children are strange aberrations. Since they see themselves as independent and unique, they go out of their way to insure that their party is different. Different it is, complete with the music of a Mozart quartet playing the best of Willie Nelson, and food provided by Wanton's, a Chinese caterer specializing in spareribs. As the onlys report the details of their gala, they smile coyly at one another.

The quirk of only children is that they are like the oldests in the life task of work, but like the youngests in terms of love and intimacy. Since they have always been the center of the universe, they expect others, and the world in general, to come to them.

As children, onlys are more affected by the economic conditions of their family of origin than other birth-order positions because any financial change in the family affected them directly. Affluence during the developmental years contributes to their sense of royalty; austerity often provokes intense striving, seriousness, and compulsiveness.

As adults, only children have little difficulty with work, while love and intimacy often create turmoil. In the work place, although they achieve, they occasionally generate strong emotions among colleagues. Some will see them as dynamic and unique (hybrid); others will see them as opinionated prima donnas who have difficulty working with others. Onlys are amazed to discover that others expect to be asked if property or responsibilities are shared. They have a difficult time imagining that others might not want to give them their time, help, and acceptance; onlys find this annoying and inconvenient, but nothing to get worked up about!

41

In short, the only child is often a mixed bag of emotions and ac-complishments—mysterious and annoying to friends, charming, and yet, on occasion, overwhelming to their parents.

Sources of Discouragement for the Only Child

Only children believe they are victimized by the classic stereotype of the "spoiled only child." Recent evidence seems to support their con-tention. The only child has problems many of us have difficulty under-standing. Most of us pit ourselves against siblings, but in the only child's world, adults are the primary source of competition. All mea-sures of success are gauged against the seemingly perfect accomplish-ments of adults.

We often hear, "S/he is so mature for his age." It is true that only children do appear overly adult for their age in their work. This is not the case where emotional relationships are concerned. Only children are capable of cooperation, but are most satisfied when they are the center of attention. They grow to expect privacy, acceptance, and compliance with their demands. Since it's rarely possible to provide these totally, onlys may feel unfairly treated. Finally, since only chil-dren compete against older people, they often entertain themselves by rebelling against authority. Oldests seek rules to follow while onlys seek rules to break.

Encouragement Strategies for Only Children

Parents of only children must avoid the temptation to confide in the child as if he or she were a mate or colleague. The child shouldn't be granted any more or less status than his/her place in the family deserves. You can satisfy the only child's need for power by giving him or her realistic responsibilities in the family without surrendering your own. In families of only three, the risk of destructive alliances is great— mother and child, for example. To avoid this, family meetings are important. Also, no matter how tempting it is, avoid using the only child as a means of manipulating your mate.

BUT THINGS CAN BE DIFFERENT

Understanding birth order can increase your empathy for the possible sources of discouragement you and your children experience. Many things can modify the child's view of his or her position: sex, family values, giftedness, age, childhood illnesses, and death of parents or siblings. All of these alter perceptions.

In the end, the most unique element of all rests in the critical mind of the beholder. One's creative power, in the final analysis, determines the life line. For example, physicians often recall early encounters with death and at the time making a commitment to overcome it; scientists often recall early childhood experiments; the physically impaired recall deciding to overcome their disability at any price. Decisions and commitments are made early, often in compensatory ways, to overcome or subvert one's situation and inadequacies.

LIFE IS ONLY SOFTLY DETERMINED

Life is only softly determined. Alternatives are as close as your perceptions and willingness to try new behavior. Cooperative kids are those who have enough courage and encouragement to do the useful thing. But kids aren't likely to learn cooperative behavior from uncooperative or discouraged adults.

SOURCES OF ADULT DISCOURAGEMENT

Far too many of us are discouraged by the ploy, "Alice's mother lets her do it," or "I am the only one who isn't allowed to go to the Boy George concert at the Sports Arena." This is a thinly veiled attack upon our parenting ability in comparison to Alice's parents. Her parents are obviously doing something we aren't or know something we don't. The insinuation is clear—they must be better parents than we are. That's discouraging!

Our sense of guilt usually unleashes a daisy chain of interfering ideas which, in turn, trigger rapid fire self-doubt. "If Mrs. A. thinks it's okay for her child to go to the concert, then maybe I'm not thinking correctly." "Will my kids be social outcasts if I don't let them go?" "Am I denying them unreasonably?" At this point we're probably

43

reconsidering our decision about the concert. But in the meantime our private second-guessing triggers overt interrogation of our children: "Why do you want to go to a concert by that nerd anyway?" "Why does Alice's mother approve?" Wrong questions all. All of us live with reality that we're not perfect as parents. But most of us live in the shadow of the fiction that if we somehow followed the prescription or plan used by other parents, we might elevate to their fictional level of excellence.

When you celebrate your imperfection instead of trying to prevent its discovery, a remarkable thing happens: you recognize that perfection is unrealistic and excessive, and then making improvements and making mistakes can be viewed positively by yourself—and understood, even loved, by your children.

Discouraged parents raise discouraged kids whose motto unfortunately becomes, "Nothing ventured, nothing lost." But if you have the courage to acknowledge your own faults, the result will be remarkable—your children will improve and so will you. You will begin to recognize courage when you see it and be amazed at the capabilities of both you and your kids. When your firstborn daughter announces that she has to go to remedial reading, instead of considering it an injunction of your stupidity, you can accept it for what it is, an encouraging, fortunate opportunity for both of you.

Giving up the myth of perfection will be a major step toward encouraging you and your children, but it will not relieve you of the necessity to discipline, guide, and teach your children. Discipline, as opposed to punishment, is much more consistent with the premise of imperfect parents and imperfect kids. You're probably wondering how—and rightfully so. *"How do I keep them in line if I don't punish them?" Wrong question. The right question is, "How do I encourage useful behavior?"*

4

PITFALLS OF PARENTING EXTREMES: Pampering Gardeners and Punitive Gatekeepers

Being imperfect is relatively easy for parents.
Admitting imperfection is harder.
— *Dolores Curran*
Traits of a Healthy Family

BRIBERY AND PUNISHMENT AREN'T DISCIPLINE

During the fifties, the only authoritative guide to parenting was Dr. Spock. The message, appropriately or inappropriately deduced, was that tender loving care—T.L.C.—was the necessary and sufficient condition for parenting. While T.L.C. is necessary, it's not sufficient and it's not discipline either.

Discipline is also necessary. Advocates of more laissez-faire parenting approaches are often confronted, as many of us are, by ornery, obnoxious kids. When Junior throws himself on the floor at the bank, the Spockian pampering gardener feels he has to stop the behavior without bruising the child's ego, his psyche, or his behind. It's predicaments like this that cause parents to bribe children off the floor. Unfortunately, this has an unhealthy reinforcing effect. Since pampering gardeners don't have the "Godfather" mentality, they make children offers that are very easy to refuse. These parents conclude, erroneously, that bribery and T.L.C. are synonymous. Furthermore, T.L.C. and bribery aren't necessary or sufficient disciplinary strategies.

More importantly, discipline and punishment are two separate and distinct activities. Discipline is education! In contrast, punishment is

45

"pain" inflicted upon someone for crimes. There is more than a nuance of difference between these two concepts. Yet parents have been confusing them for decades and acting as if they're one and the same thing. They aren't, and it's important to distinguish between the two.

Punishment—pain inflicted for crimes—is often measured in terms of the child's pain threshold. If the child is hurting, the punishment is working; if the child isn't hurting, it isn't working. Unfortunately kids who are physically or emotionally punished absorb the blow along with the message, "Might is right." Or "When I am big enough and strong enough I can hurt others like I've been hurt."

Pampering gardeners and punitive gatekeepers both generally raise tyrants. Tyranny means "absolute rule, arbitrary or despotic exercise of power." And yes, children can be tyrants. If there is any doubt about this definition, consider the four-year-old girl at the supermarket who spots the candy at the checkout stand, strategically placed at eye level for four-year-olds, and falls to the floor in a thrashing rage, in an emotional maneuver to get the candy. Mom or Dad may hold her gently, buy the candy, or swat her. In some cases desperate and indecisive parents might try all three techniques.

PAMPERING GARDENERS SOW SEEDS OF TYRANNY

As the movies have shown us—what sells demands a sequel. In an airport recently, I watched one episode that might well be titled, "Raiders of the Long Concourse."

Directly across from me sat a mother and her two sons; the youngest sat restlessly between the mother and older brother. Mom sternly warned, "Watch your brother while I get cigarettes." No sooner said, little brother darted out onto the concourse to the loud admonitions of the eldest, "Stop, Brad, stop!" Spinning on spiked heels, Mom bounded down the concourse in hot pursuit, purse flapping, cigarettes falling, and one hand reaching out for the catch.

Junior was in full stride, and Mom was trying to reach hers while smiling apologetically at those unsuspecting travelers she lumbered into from time to time. It's not easy sprinting on a marble floor in high heels, with a smile on your face. Mom overtook Junior at the "up" escalator and plucked him off the floor like a large crane, wheels spinning.

Returning to the boarding area appearing slightly cyanotic, Mom softly and insistently offered Junior a fistful of mints, "Here, you'll like these." Accepting the bribe, Junior picked at the mints half-heartedly. As the color returned to Mother's cheeks, her attention shifted from her son to her book. As her attention wandered, so did Junior. By the time she had turned the first page, Junior headed back down the concourse on a dead run.

The whole episode was replayed three times before boarding, and by that time the only thing Mother could do was ask for oxygen. Each time they returned to the boarding area she upped the ante—more mints. On the last occasion she instructed big brother to buy a Coke and candy bar to keep Junior busy. Mom wasn't able to see the purposefulness of his behavior, much less generate disciplinary alternatives.

She had grown used to trying to buy her son's good behavior. When for some inexplicable reason bribery failed, she assumed his needs were urgent—he was in desperate need of affection, or that "he was just going through a 'stage'." Parents endure more agony in the name of a "stage" than is reasonable or sensible. Junior forced her to endure the tyrannical performance. Exclusive tender loving care or emotional and physical bribery are the early forerunners of extortion, childhood edicts, and juvenile dictatorship. A bribe is just a euphemism for coercion. It's rarely effective and never discipline.

PUNITIVE GATEKEEPERS ALSO PRODUCE TYRANNY

Under very similar circumstances while flying, I observed a mother and daughter sitting in the smoking section of the airplane. The little girl, about six years old, had protested throughout boarding procedures about where she wanted to sit. She didn't want to sit with Mother "in all that smoke." Unfortunately, since they were traveling alone, Mother's options appeared limited. Push came to shove and once airborne, the little girl generated one little power struggle after another. "Stop picking in those ashtrays...Keep your seat either up or down...Leave the ice cubes in the glass," etc. With each episode, the bickering grew more intense. Finally, Mother issued the ultimatum and repeated it three times, "If you don't stop, I'll spank you."

No sooner had she made her proclamation than the daughter launched her turkey loaf into her mother's coffee. Mom promptly began swatting her between the tray tables. As Mom wrestled for leverage, she dumped her own meal in the aisle, bringing the flight attendants. Throughout it all, the daughter wailed so loudly that one elderly woman in front thought the plane was going down. So what's the moral—Don't spank 'em when you are in the air? Not exactly. Here it is: That which you seek to accomplish through the use of physical punishment, control of the child, is the thing you are least likely to attain. Within the first three rows of this spectacle, few were amused, but the further away from the action one was, the broader the smiles. Prophetically, the more we are able to remove ourselves from these struggles, the more amusing they become.

The futility of trying to control through physical power was demonstrated exquisitely by this unfortunate woman. And, in a sense, the impact that punitive methods have on families and communities was shown in microcosm during the flight. The child, whose rights should have been considered at the outset, exerted her power over her mother and the rest of the adult establishment.

PITFALLS OF BRIBERY AND PUNISHMENT

We're able to laugh at these episodes because they mirror aspects of our own behavior—we recognize the frustration, theirs as well as our own. Also, the classic myths and pitfalls of bribery and punishment as parenting strategies are revealed. In the first encounter, the parent mistakenly assumed that if she nurtured and rewarded a youngster, all would be well. The results proved otherwise.

For the last decade psychologists researching behavior modification have been telling us that proper reinforcements offered at the appropriate time will modify any behavior. Isn't this true? Not entirely! For subtle but significant reasons, reinforcement theory developed by studying pigeons and rats fails with those of us who have skin but no feathers. Pavlov gave us a clue as to why. Roughly paraphrased, he said the transference of conditioning principles from animals to humans is problematic for one critical reason. Humans, unlike any other animal, possess a "second signal" system, written language. This second signal system reflects our self-consciousness, our ability to reflect upon our fate, style, goals, emotions, and purposes. To assume that an "M & M" or a mint will sufficiently reinforce a human being is overly simplistic.

Broke Brokers

These are pretty esoteric reasons for rejecting reward or bribery strategies, but there are far more pragmatic reasons. Not long ago while conducting a group for parents of adolescents, a parent voiced a concern about his son. His son, who was a junior in high school, had issued his parents an ultimatum, "Unless you buy me a Corvette for graduation, I won't graduate with honors."

This kind of tyranny usually spawns the wrong question: "How could a seventeen-year-old make such an outrageous statement?" The right question is: "How have we fostered such materialistic tyranny?" In this case, Mom and Dad both had a great deal invested in education, intelligence, and success. During grade school they began offering five dollars for B's and ten dollars for A's. By the time the boy was in the fifth grade, the amount had reached 20 and 30 dollars, respectively. By the time the boy was a sophomore in high school, the amount of revenue generated in a single grading period exceeded the windfall profits of most oil companies.

For most of us, this wouldn't be an issue because we couldn't afford it. But actually no one can afford to move his or her children through material contingencies or rewards. There are several reasons why. First, if you hope to have an impact, the reward must be significant. As children become more sophisticated, they up the proverbial stakes. No matter how wealthy, parents are easily bankrupted by the demands of children. Second, by providing rewards for a task, the task itself becomes secondary. Children perform based on monetary reward, not personal improvement or cooperation with others.

Third, in all likelihood the task at hand is one that Mom and Dad have more invested in than the child does. When this happens, parents are on the losing end of the bargain. If parents invest more in the desired behavior than children do, they are destined to be manipulated. Fourth, in order to have an effective system of reinforcement, it must be offered "every time there is a successful approximation of the target behavior."

The performance of a task must always be judged for quality by the reinforcer/parent. In the process the child becomes controlled and motivated by another person rather than self. In short, kids learn to do only those things they are paid to do. Then we're baffled by their greed. In the business world motivation by reward may have value, but not as much as one would expect. In personal relationships, families, and marriages, it has virtually no survival value.

HERE COMES THE JUDGE

Think of the vigilance required on your part. You're the investigator, the enforcer, and finally the judge. In order for rewards to be dispensed, a one up/one down relationship must exist. The parent passes judgment upon the child and extends worth based upon performance. "Good boy, John, you made an A." Is the reverse true? If John doesn't get an A is he a bad boy? The kid thinks so. It's a case of child as "Golden Retriever." The kid's worth becomes conditional, conditional upon the evaluation of others. Conditional worth reduces the kid's status from person to pet. In short, when parents use praise with the intent to manipulate children, they are employing what I call "pet praise."

Pet Praise

Ironically, "pet praise" doesn't produce cooperative behavior—it fosters persistent pests. Children assume that if they persist long enough on a particular course they just might be rewarded even if they're disruptive. Their perceptions are accurate, but their behavior is useless. It's as if they are waiting for a payoff by the parental slot machine: they never know when the machine is going to hit so they stand at the machine of misbehavior for hours, days, or weeks. Eventually it pays.

Ironically, the more persistent children are, the more it seems to pay. So, why not try a tantrum in the check-out lane of the supermarket—it worked last week! Unknowingly parents have contributed to the child's habitual behavior and they pay through the nose. A classic cartoon depicts response conditioning: One rat says to the other, "I've really got this guy trained. Every time I press this bar he gives me food." Who controls whom?

Parent as Enforcer

Now that bribery has been dispensed with as a disciplinary tactic you might ask, "What about punishment? It isn't education either." Recall for a moment the definition of punishment in this case—it is inflicting

50

pain or penalty for wrongdoing. If certain principles are followed, punishment does accomplish something. First, it must be swift and direct and immediately follow the transgression. Second, it must be administered upon each and every occasion the misbehavior occurs. Third, the punishment must be substantial enough to deter the misbehavior. If you are able to implement these principles consistently, you might stop certain behaviors, but then again you might not. Punishment might stop a behavior—if you're strong enough to break the child's pain threshold. But even if you are temporarily strong enough to break the child's pain threshold, this must not be construed as education or discipline. Punishment may stop disturbing behavior, but it will never teach new cooperative, responsible behavior.

There are psychologists who suggest that punishment is effective if done properly. One expert says pinching the trapezius muscle is pretty helpful. However, you may be twice your child's age but half his size—then where do you pinch him? Also, in using punishment as a motivational tactic, adults run the risk of accidentally teaching children that when they are big enough and strong enough, they are entitled to punish others.

Perhaps the most devastating outcome of the use of punishment is demonstrated in maximum security penitentiaries where 80 percent of the population were abused as children by adults who couldn't distinguish between pinching the trapezius muscles and beating.

Shortcomings of bribery:

1. Larger and larger payoffs are required to induce the behavior desired.
2. The rewards provided often minimize the importance of a task, subordinating its significance.
3. Children become externally motivated and lose internal motivation.
4. Rewards often establish power relationships between adults and children.

Shortcomings of punishment:

1. Autocratic approaches instill the value that "might makes right."
2. Punitive tactics usually fail to teach the child positive new behaviors.

3. Punishment always establishes a battleground for power and competition between parent and child.

Now, having been told not to bribe or punish—or having failed after trying either or both—you may feel at a loss. You're probably asking, "What's left?" The wrong question springs into mind: "Since bribery and punishment don't work, how can I control the child?" The right question ought to be: "How can I educate and encourage useful behavior and control myself and the situation?" Another way to phrase this is: *"If we don't bribe or punish, what is left?" The answer: "Encouragement and educational discipline."*

Discipline

Discipline, after all, is education. It's moral, physical, and cognitive training. A radio announcer recently asked, "How do we whip kids into shape these days?" If "whip" suggests driving kids against their will, it's not possible figuratively or literally. Moral education, or discipline, involves much more than the whip, strap, or bribe. To be truly effective, adults have to lead, not command their children in the ways of society.

HOW TO BE AN ENCOURAGING PARENT

Leading, then, involves several critical components. First, to lead effectively adults must model, recognize, and encourage cooperative behavior—behavior that constitutes good citizenship and contributes to the family. Second, in this technologically advanced era we must find or create opportunities for kids to make significant contributions to their family and community. Third, to lead we must win, not command, the respect of our kids. Winning the respect of kids means communicating and treating them with the same respect we want. Finally, to lead and discipline, we must allow children to assume responsibility for their actions. As hard as this might be for us, we must allow them to overcome adversity and, when necessary, provide opportunities for them to struggle a little. All four of these conditions must be met for children to be "disciplined," that is, for them to become courageous, responsible, and cooperative.

Given the technological advances—dishwashers, microwave ovens, crock pots, refrigerators with brains, as well as a host of other conveniences—adversity is going to be tough to find. Further, what technology doesn't do for kids, we usually do. Our toughest job as parents is being helpful without stripping kids of responsibility and strength—being helpers, not stretcher bearers.

PART TWO

STRATEGIES FOR ENCOURAGEMENT

5

NEVER DO FOR CHILDREN WHAT THEY CAN DO FOR THEMSELVES

Children's courage can be measured by their opportunity to overcome adversity.

—F.M.

"How do we encourage our children? It's clear from the preceding chapters that we can't punish or bribe, so what's left?" In a word—encouragement. According to Webster, it means, "to inspire with courage, spirit, or hope; to animate; hearten; cheer on or up; to help or give patronage; to foster." To be encouraging as a parent is to do all of these and more.

You might conclude that encouragement is no more than a good dose of tender loving care. On the contrary, encouragement is a good deal more. There are three major components involved: attitude, technique, and communication.

ENCOURAGING ATTITUDES

If you look carefully at the definition of encouragement, you find absolutely no hint of praise, reinforcement, payment, or reward. However, behavioral psychology has led us, mistakenly, to believe that to praise, pay, or reward is to inspire. As a result, parenting strategies become a system of payoffs. The trouble is, after years of token economics we find that we are dealing with a generation of children and young adults who do for one another only when paid.

Children are astounded when they are asked to do family chores without pay. When parents are insightful enough to point out that adults are not paid to perform these same tasks, kids are indignant. The conclusion is clear—encouraging parents must introduce a new ethic. They must highlight the fact that membership in the family produces rights, privileges, and *responsibilities*.

To be truly encouraging as a parent, it's essential to believe two things about your children. First, that children are capable—far more capable then we believe. If you take what you think children can do and double it, you'll be half right. Therefore, you must begin to believe that *children can handle it*. They may not handle things as neatly, quickly, or cleverly as you might—but they *can* handle them.

The second belief is this: one's worth and dignity ought not be tied exclusively to one's capacity to live up to the expectations and rewards of others. It's difficult to say which of these two ideas is most critical. Both are essential to healthy personality development. The messages for parents in each are direct, but not necessarily easy to accept or practice. They are: 1) have faith in the child's ability; and 2) separate the deed from the doer in terms of dignity and worth.

Have Faith in the Child

Having faith in a child's abilities is a heartening and relieving experience. Once convinced of this, you are equipped to withdraw unneeded attention, service, reprimands, and protection. The children of the Depression years demonstrated the point. As a group, their coping skills are legend. Having the "opportunity to overcome adversity" is a tremendous asset and crucial in developing responsibility. Much has been made of the debilitating effect our cultural affluence has had on families, and therefore there is much to be said for adversity.

Assuming that a child is capable incorporates opportunities for responsibility and discipline. These notions are not tender-minded ideas of the sixties but firm, fair, democratic alternatives for parents of the eighties. Parents often say, "We want to provide things for our kids we didn't have!" What haven't you had? If you reflect a bit, you'll discover that you went without very little and probably savored those times you had to work for something you wanted.

Hard work and adversity, then, have a lot of potential as training vehicles. Allowances, for example, are always problematic for parents. Clever guidelines have been established for this by psychologist Manford Sonstegard, and these will be expanded as we address techniques of encouragement. However, a brief guideline is to provide less than the child needs—significantly less. Not less emotionally or intellectually, but less materially.

Separate the Deed from the Doer

As mentioned earlier, behavioral psychology would have us believe that cooperative behavior is simply produced by appropriately rendered reinforcement. The absurdity of these token techniques may be seen if you try to place yourself in the following vignette:

You have just finished sweeping the kitchen floor and your mate arrives and sees you finishing the job. Your mate says, "Good boy/girl, John/Jane. You did a nice job. You're a good mate. Good job." You are probably laughing or feeling resentment because you're able to make an emotional connection between this story and the "pet praise" described earlier in chapter four. This is clearly a case of spouse as golden retriever; a case in which a person, spouse or child, is treated as if s/he were externally motivated and controlled by material or emotional tokens; a case of "pet praise."

What's wrong with this exchange between marital partners? If you are able to place yourself on the receiving end of pet praise, you experience several things: 1) the superficial nature of the remark, given your level of competence and the relative ease of sweeping the floor; 2) annoying feelings of inferiority created by someone determining your dignity and worth ("good boy/girl") based upon your performance of a superficial or routine chore; and 3) a sense of resentment supported by the fact that the speaker's actions seem to assume that you will perform the job again simply to receive the reinforcement they provided.

Adult to adult, this exchange makes you feel like you're a fool who doesn't have brains enough to do the job or realize that you're being conned. It would be more absurd if we expected our spouse to pay us. "Here's a nice steak dinner—that'll be $14.90." Paying for family membership or cooperation is ludicrous, of course. But thousands of parents pay their children to do things they will never be paid for as

59

adults, spouses, and parents. The point is that as adults much of what we do for our families is done because of internal motivation, but we're raising our children assuming that they can only be externally motivated.

Encouraging Alternatives

Let's consider the previous episode from an encouraging perspective. "John/Jane, thanks for doing the floor. I appreciate it. There will be less for us to do tonight and that will be nice. Is there anything I can do to help?" There are about the same number of words as before, but it's different! The focus and purpose of our remarks have changed in several ways: 1) the speaker has expressed appreciation for the effort made rather than judging adequacy of performance and awarding dignity based upon the evaluation; 2) the speaker focuses upon the contribution our actions made to the family rather than evaluating our "goodness"; 3) finally, the speaker assumes that the other person is of equal dignity and worth, no matter if he or she sweeps the floor or not. Dignity and worth was acknowledged and there was no element of judgment involved. Now that's encouraging! Encouragement is distinctly different from behavior-specific praise (pet praise) and generates vastly different motivation and behavior.

Dr. Dreikurs was fond of saying, "A child needs encouragement like a plant needs water." And reciprocally, discouragement is the fuel for useless goals. To reverse the process, to dissolve mischievous behavior, parents must encourage their kids and one another. Our objectives, then, are to communicate encouragement to our mates and kids.

Techniques of Encouragement

Almost all interactions that occur between parents and kids could be encouraging, discipline included. The following guidelines help generalize these principles to many circumstances:

1. Recognize and focus on assets and strengths.
2. Provide opportunities for the child to make legitimate contributions by asking for his/her help and providing regular responsibilities.

3. Suggest small steps to accomplish tasks when young children need help. The entire job may seem overwhelming to the youngster.

4. Notice effort regardless of the level of competence displayed.

5. Use humor. Humor is often an effective tool for encouraging acceptance of self and imperfection. Additionally, it allows an individual to own or personalize failure as well as success. It is a major component in the counseling process for both couples and families.

6. Take time for training. At neutral times (not during the heat of battle) provide instruction, advice, and guidance in new tasks. These can include learning to run the washing machine or balancing a checkbook.

7. Spend time with the child. Particular attention will be devoted to this in a later chapter.

8. Listen to the child and make it obvious you are listening.

9. Mind your own business. Allow children to solve their own problems.

10. Don't emphasize liabilities. It is quite easy to be critical, but it is far more challenging to be constructive and helpful.

11. Provide opportunities for success. Offer opportunities for responsibilities in areas where the child has a chance to succeed.

Words of Encouragement

Encouraging responsible behavior often hinges on offering the right words. The following are offered as possible examples of encouraging language.

1. "Thanks, that was a big help. I appreciate it."

2. "I'll bet you feel good about that."

3. "It feels neat to know something well."

4. "I'll bet that made you feel good."

5. "It sure made me feel good for us to work together."

6. "It was nice solving this together."

7. "I'm not sure what we would have done without your help. We really needed your help."

8. "It feels good when we share responsibilities."

9. "You're really getting good at that. It must feel good."

10. "That was a great effort. I'm sure next time it will be even better."

11. "That was a clever idea. I wish I had thought of it."

12. "You really thought that through well. It shows."

13. "I'm sure you can solve it."

14. "You'll make it."

15. "That was a nice choice. You really look nice."

16. "That was very thoughtful. Thank you."

17. "You have certainly improved."

18. "I can tell you have thought this through. Why don't you give it a try?"

19. "That must have hurt. Let me know if I can help."

20. "That didn't work out very well. I am wondering what we can learn from it."

21. "You recognize your mistake and that ought to help you next time."

22. "I could sure use your help if you could find the time."

23. "We really love you, but we really dislike what you're doing."

24. "That's an interesting idea. I wonder what will happen if you do it?"

25. "Hang in there. I know you'll get it."

26. "It sounds like you want us to think you can't handle it, but we have faith in you. We know you can."

27. "Nice job. I am really happy for you."

28. "I love you."

While this list may be helpful as a primer, there is really only one thing that you need to remember. The words you use aren't critical, but your attitude is. If your intention is to subtly manipulate your child, then what you say will amount to pet praise. However, if you have really come to believe that children can handle it, and your objective is to encourage responsibility, what you say will be encouraging.

If you believe that your kids are people and not pets, then you'll want to communicate *with* and not *to* them. That's the difference between encouraging, two-way communication, and discouraging, door-slamming monologues. Parents should be able to communicate with their kids at any age. Unfortunately most of us lose touch with our kids much too soon. All too often kids become "deaf" very early—at about 18 months of age. It seems like they really don't hear. Eventually we learn that kids are not really deaf, just "adult deaf." They have learned to tune kids in and tune us out.

ENCOURAGING COMMUNICATION

Listening

Playing deaf or choosing what to hear is an attempt to get a payoff for two useless goals—attention and power. Children routinely ignore what parents say because they know it will be said again, and again—and again. And, each repetition will be a little louder than the last. Youngsters learn that Mom and Dad aren't really serious until the pronouncement is repeated for the fifteenth time at a deafening level.

Parents who pride themselves on being reasonable and intelligent often think their lecturettes are understood and accepted by their children. Have you ever wondered whether your favorite dialogue works with your kids? If you think it does, ask yourself how many times you've repeated yourself. You probably have had the same "talk" dozens of times.

Curiously, those of us who see ourselves as cerebral are the slowest to make the connection—or lack of it—between an adult's conversation and a child's behavior. If you have a high priority on thinking, reasoning, and doing the "right" thing, you probably talk incessantly. In your most reasonable voice, you chide, "Haven't we talked about this?" Of course. But what the youngster has deduced from the talk is that when his/her behavior becomes obnoxious, you'll *talk* about it. Children, being the astute observers that they are, watch us very carefully; then they draw conclusions based on our actions, not on our words.

Giving sermonettes may gratify your sense of nobility and fit the myth of perfect parenthood, but they also reward the child's useless bid for attention. If you cherish your sermonettes, tape them and replay them when you have a real need to hear yourself. Then you're free to continue working on more useful things, but still have the benefit of listening to yourself. And, since you're far more impressed by your speeches than your kids are, you have done justice to the sermonette.

On the other hand, if you question the veracity of your own speeches after hearing them a time or two, you may want to consider abandoning them. Giving up sermonettes will not be easy. Initially, you will be oblivious to the frequency, intensity, and duration of your tirades. Your partner can be of help here. Give your spouse permission to clandestinely record one of your favorite diatribes. You will treat yourself to an introspective experience and discover what your spouse and kids have been unable to tell you for years.

One mother who couldn't stop sermonizing or bring herself to record herself was lucky enough to have the following exchange with her small daughter. As Mom busily pored over a law brief, her small daughter strolled through the family room pushing her doll's baby carriage. Suddenly the little girl stopped and leaned angrily into the carriage. "Dammit, Polly, lie down. You know better than that!" Mom gasped, "Beth, you know better than that! You shouldn't talk like that." Without missing a step or beat Beth whimsically responded, "Oh, Mom, it's okay. I'm the Mom now!" Ouch! Our children are usually a mirror of our own emotion and dialect. When your child's reflection of you is painfully accurate and embarrassing, it's time to clean up your side of the mirror. Begin by closing your mouth and observing the competence your youngsters possess. You will be encouraged and, in turn, encourage your youngsters.

In order to prevent withdrawal symptoms that accompany closing your mouth cold turkey, try the following phrase, "You can handle it." When said in a firm, encouraging tone, the results are often remarkable. Having uttered this little phrase, you may not have to say anything else.

Closing your mouth is a big decision. Don't take it lightly! If you don't mind repeating things five times or more, find it easier to do things yourself, and believe kids are deaf or simply not able, don't try it. Or, if you use your speeches as a vehicle for pulling your spouse into your service, or inducing guilt, don't make the sacrifice. Most important of all, if you wonder how you will be needed if you stop talking, hold off on this recommendation.

On the other hand, if you have worked through these sacrifices and think you have the courage to find a spot in your family without being Oral Roberts or Joan of Arc, give it a try. All you have to gain are responsive, respectful children.

Avoiding Ice Cream Responses

Obviously you can't be mute captives in your own home, but if you expect to be heard by your children you have to listen. That isn't as simple as it sounds. Communication among families is a complicated business and many people have spent a lifetime studying family communication styles. But you don't need a lecture on the intricacies of family communication, just pragmatic tactics for improving yours.

There are at least two levels or messages transmitted in every communication, especially between parents and kids. On one level there is the content of the message being sent; and on the other there is the emotional intention of the message. The content is the "stuff" the conversation is about—the subject. The emotion expresses the speaker's private convictions about how life *ought* to be, for example how power ought to be dispensed in the family. In the case below, Kristin hasn't practiced her piano and mother begins to nag her about it:

> Mom: "When are you going to practice piano?"
> Kristin: "I'll do it after dinner."
> Mom: "You won't have enough time to do your chores then."
> Kristin: "It's not enough to practice. I have to practice when you want me to and be happy doing it!"
> Mom: "Don't talk to me that way. You'll do as you're told or else."
> At this point Dad joins the confrontation.
> Dad: "Kristin, you know you don't talk to your mother that way, but, Mom, I think she would have time to get things done after dinner."

In this case the content is about piano lessons, but the emotion is about who is entitled to boss whom. Although Mom believes that she is entitled to boss the children, Kristin realizes that her father doesn't hold to this view. Therefore, Kristin is willing to misbehave and even risk reprimand, if she can get Dad to join her against Mom. The content of the communication is about piano lessons, but the emotional process is about the distribution of power. In communication the emotional level is not about "things," but about how we control one another.

Our style of exchanging content and emotional messages with our children establishes a major part of what could be called a relationship style. Simply put, our private convictions about how power is distributed and how life ought to be are balanced with, or pitted against, our children's private convictions about these same issues. Our private, or emotional, convictions set the tone, style and pattern of our relationships. For example, if we say on one level that children ought to be responsible and independent, but privately believe that children are incapable and irresponsible, then our communication with them will be defined by this incongruence. *We will lecture them about responsibility and independence but insist, emotionally, that they do only what they're told to do!* How can they do both? By expressing one thing while privately believing another, parents place children in a double bind.

In the face of this incongruence children develop means of walking this tight rope. They may attempt a balancing act, ignore both messages, or act on one while sabotaging the other. For example, Kristin responded to the content of Mom's question, "I'll do it after dinner..." knowing full well that she was emotionally challenging Mom. Kristin's communication acknowledged the content of her mother's message, but railed at Mom's private conviction that Kristin must be told what to do.

The relationship between Kristin and her mother becomes defined in terms of the emotional dance they do with one another. "I'll lead." "No, I'll lead." "No. I'll lead." In this case the relationship has become defined as combative, argumentative, and competitive. Each partner struggles for supremacy by using similar emotional power tactics. In other circumstances relationships are defined by different emotional styles. Therefore, the content is important in communication but the emotion is critical.

In order to really communicate with their kids, parents must bring the content and emotion of their communication in line. Most people, not just parents, are prone to close doors rather than open them when attempting to communicate; they shut off or close communication. Sometimes the door slams shut and sometimes it slowly swings closed. Door-closing behavior is easier to recognize than it is to change.

Several years ago I saw a graphic example of door-slamming communication while I was supervising a beginning counselor trainee. Her first client was a genuinely frightened sixteen-year-old girl. The following is an excerpt from their first session:

> Jeff and I went to the homecoming dance last fall and we stopped with the gang to have ice cream at the Dairy Bar. We had malts and danced some more and had lots of fun. Then Jeff and I drove out to the dam and parked. We got into things pretty heavy and before either one of us knew it we were doing "it." That was three months ago and I haven't had my period since. I don't know what to do...Jeff and I aren't even going out anymore. That was the first and only time we had sex.
>
> There was a long silence and then finally the rookie counselor sputtered "What...what kind of ice cream did you have?"

From that day forward I've called these utterances "ice cream responses." Any response by an adult which ignores the significant content and emotion of a message is an ice cream response. If the listener fails to hear the emotional message, s/he slams the door shut. In the case above, the emotional message was in part, "I am frightened to death and it has taken a lot of courage for me to come to you with this. My life is out of my control; others must provide direction for me." This young woman's emotion expressed fear and confusion plus her private conviction that "Life is uncontrollable and help comes from outside myself."

Door closers are usually questions, closed questions—questions that require only yes or no answers and always *ignore content and emotion*. Example: "My English teacher doesn't like me and she grades me unfairly. No matter how good my paper is, she tears it apart." Adult response: "Do you proofread your work?" Bang! The doorway to communication just slammed shut.

Door-slamming communicators have a number of characteristics in common. Some of these include:

1. Knowing in advance what the speaker is going to say and ignoring 50 percent of what is said.

2. Focusing on one aspect of what the person has said and ignoring the overall message of the speaker.

3. Rejecting the speaker's words as insignificant, simple, or uninteresting. This can be accomplished by disqualifying the speaker through inattentiveness, picking finger nails as they speak, doodling, etc. Or, the speaker can be disqualified by direct rebuttal, "You don't understand the issues, it's this way..." "Your idea may have worked before but this is a more involved (sophisticated) problem, so it isn't going to work here."

4. Providing the speaker with "emotional cookies" which minimize the importance of the speaker's message in a covertly condescending manner. Parents want desperately to do something for their kids when they are in trouble or a new learning situation, but most of the time they discount the importance of the problem situation to the child.

   For example, Susie says: "Mom, Lisa and Jenny made friends with me and then deliberately used what I told them against me."

   Mom replies: "Dear, kids your age always have those problems. Just call Kathy and play with her today. By tomorrow everyone will have forgotten about it."

   An emotional cookie is any gesture that discounts the child's concerns or supplies superficial advice as a means of distracting the child from his or her concerns. The message communicated through such emotional cookies is, "Things like this don't really matter." The child feels discounted and insignificant.

To keep the lines of communication open, to get your message across, you will have to insure that you hear your children. *Children who listen have parents who do!* These parents have several communication skills which focus on content and process.

1. They commit themselves to listening.

2. They physically prepare themselves to listen. They attend to the speaker, turn off the television set, put down their magazine, and listen.

3. They wait for the speaker to complete his/her sentence and avoid cutting the speaker off in mid-sentence, anticipating the conclusion of his/her statement.

4. Good listeners use their analytical skills to supplement, not replace, what they are hearing.

Characteristically, people prepare their responses to what a speaker is saying while s/he is still talking. In adult-child relationships this can be lethal because the parent loses half of what the child says and the child quickly becomes resentful.

One certain way to slam the door in any conversation is to launch an interrogation. Even the innocent feel offended and react angrily. The red flags which signal interrogation are, again, questions which must be answered yes or no. It only takes a couple of these yes-no questions to make the child feel interrogated and to slam the door on open communication. As soon as the child senses the third degree s/he tunes out.

Getting the "Stuff" Right

The content of communication—the "stuff" being talked about—can be easily misunderstood, distorted, or interpreted to meet our own agenda. As a result, it's important to hear accurately, to get the child's message straight. This amounts to listening with an accurate and fair ear.

Content skills are easy to develop with practice. The content (subject) is easy because that is the "topic" of your conversation. The child's emotional agenda focuses on the how and why of the message. The easiest guideline for understanding this underlying meaning is to ask yourself why the child has an emotional need to tell you what he or she is telling you. Also, why is s/he telling you this in this manner? (Remember: understanding why doesn't mean asking why with yes-no questions!) If you can identify the child's emotional needs as these occur, you can attend to both the *what* message and the *why*, or emotional purpose of the message. The skills listed below increase your ability to attend to the emotional purpose and content of the child's message.

1. Seek meaning instead of interrogating. Try to seek the child's meaning or interpretation of the situation. Do this by simply reflecting the statement, and most importantly, the emotion of what the child said. Admittedly this isn't always as simple as it sounds.

> "I sense you're arguing with me about this stuff when what you're trying to tell me is that you're capable of making this decision without my help."

"You expect perfection from yourself and when you don't achieve it you would rather quit than accept second best."

"You feel unfairly judged."

Don't reach too far beyond what the child has said and don't be judgmental. "You're telling me you can make this decision by yourself because you know more about what's going on than we do." Or, "You think you're ready for this decision but you're not. Tomorrow you'll see I am right."

2. Give support. Validate your youngster's emotions by labeling them and letting the child know s/he is entitled to those emotions.

> "You're confused and frightened of losing your respect, but you're also frightened of losing your relationship with him/her."

> "You feel like your Mom and I do things to you at times so we will look good as parents—you're right, we do."

3. Voice observations. Express your observations in a nonjudgmental way by using "I" messages and owning your own emotions.

> "I get very angry when I see your boy/girlfriend treating you with less respect than I think you deserve."

> "I see a lot of stuff lying around the living room and it belongs to all of us. Can we try to come to some agreement about what to do about it?"

4. Disclose your emotions. You are entitled to your own emotions and it's important that your children know how you feel, but it's critical to make a distinction between how you feel and the child's behavior. You may feel a particular way, but the child shouldn't be blamed or held responsible for your feelings.

> "It hurts me when you yell at your mother and are disrespectful to her. I dislike it because I love both of you."

> "When I have to pick your belongings up from my bedroom, I get angry because I don't think it's fair."

5. Seek alternatives. When the problem is the child's, the solution must be his or hers, not yours. However, you can help the child generate alternatives.

> "It sounds like several things have occurred to you. How about talking through each of them with me and see how they feel to you. You think that you could stop seeing him altogether but the abruptness of that might cause more problems than you have now. How would it create problems? Let's talk about the pros and cons to see which you could live with and which you couldn't."

> "I can see why you feel the way that you do. Let's say you go ahead with your plan. If you were Mr. Blank, what would you do to you in return?"

Trying to learn how to communicate openly by reading about it is like trying to learn how to mountain climb from a book. Explanations are necessary but not sufficient. In short, you have to practice and learn by your successes. One simple but straightforward method of helping you hone your skills is to tape record your family meetings; replay them and you'll get immediate feedback about how well you hear your kids.

Being Heard

A simple approach to clearly communicating your own content and emotion is to admit to your own emotions and communicate your business about family rules openly. There are four simple techniques which can help you improve your consistency and assume better ownership of your emotional intentions. These guidelines sharpen your communication skills and provide a structure for sharing your perceptions and emotions with children without blaming or interrogating.

1. *"Ask two questions" rule*—A simple but helpful technique to avoid the interrogation syndrome is the "ask two questions" rule. If you must ask questions, ask more than one before you launch your rebuttal. Here's a comparative example. Most of us open with a question as a means of setting up our rebuttal.

   Parent: Why are you still seeing him?
   Child: Sometimes he's fun!
   Parent: I wish you'd give him up. He never treats you right.

When a question must be asked it's better to precede it with a self statement and avoid the obvious yes-no set up.

Parent: I have been thinking a lot about you today. How have you and Bob been getting along?

Child: We're still seeing each other but things have cooled off a lot.

Parent: I'm not sure I'm hearing disappointment or anger. How did things get to this point between you?

You'll notice something different about the second set of questions. The questions are open and yet not interrogative. The questions are not yes-no, nor do they ask why. "Why" is interrogative and immediately places the child on the defensive. It requires the person to justify his/her actions. "Why" questions are best left to counselors or therapists and should be discouraged between spouses or parents and kids. Ask two "how" questions before generating a response. By using this technique you may not only communicate a desire to understand, you may actually understand better.

2. *"Make I statements" rule*—Another rule of good listening is to make "I" statements and not "you" statements. For example, "I get very angry when I have to be responsible for reminding you to practice the piano."

"You" statements usually indict the speaker: "You always say that and you really make me angry!" Good communicators lead with "I" statements which tend to demonstrate their ownership of emotions.

3. *"Avoid the past" rule*—Another guideline for good communication is to stick to the issues at hand. Here's an example where the parent focuses the issue on the present.

Child: You never let me do anything! You didn't let me go to the Madonna concert and now I don't suppose you'll let me go to this either.

Parent: I know you felt that was unfair but let's talk about this concert. Maybe the circumstances are different.

This avoids past transgressions and attempts to keep things in the present tense.

4. *"Make requests, not demands" rule*—Effective communicators make requests and not demands, framing their requests with "I would like," instead of "I need" statements. "I am going to be working late tomorrow night, and I had planned to have a roast.

We could eat as scheduled if you would be willing to turn it on when you get home from school and check it once or twice. Could you give me a hand?" In this situation the child has a legitimate opportunity to say no, but the consequences will affect him or her as well as everyone else. If the child says no, the outcome will be inconvenient but not catastrophic. A more typical but less effective way to handle the situation is this: "I have to work late so if we're going to eat on time, you're going to have to turn on the roast." The child feels less like cooperating because he has no choice.

Employing these simple rules for communication gives you a good chance of coordinating the content and emotion of your message and also hearing your child's. Communication can be open, reasonable, pleasant, and democratic. Practice these skills with your family, and you'll find that people can disagree without being disagreeable.

THEY CAN HANDLE IT!

As reasonable as the above message sounds, you still may be saying, "I want proof positive that my kids are capable of handling responsibility and adversity." That's understandable, but for the most part your kids have already been demonstrating, day in and day out, how competent they are. Yet, you aren't willing or able to believe in their ability. Even when youngsters demonstrate competence that flies in the face of the adults' private logic, parents don't let reality interfere with their perceptions.

Let's try to provide a few examples of childhood competence that might illuminate your private logic about children's inadequacies. For example, you may have been responsible for the weekly washing of your oldest son's baseball uniform because you've assumed he knows nothing about operating the washing machine. Then you stumble on the fact that all along your son has been doing his own uniform a second time for the mid-week practice. Your emotional reaction might be, "Wow, how could I believe for so long that he was incapable!" Your discovery is confusing because it challenges your entrenched assumptions about adequacy—yours and the child's. You have assumed for years that the child can't and won't get along without you.

In my own case I've fallen victim to such underestimation at the expense of my kids. Recently, my two daughters were taking care of a litter of kittens for friends who were away on vacation. At the evening feeding the mother cat escaped from the neighbors' house. There was much fretting, commanding, and suggesting on my part about calling the veterinarian to arrange bottle feeding the kittens, etc. Eventually we all retired after midnight and I stewed.

At 7:15 A.M. I went upstairs to check on things. To my surprise, the girls had taken turns setting their alarms beginning at 4:30 A.M. and had already found the cat and returned her to her litter. I was struck by the cooperation, creativity, and responsibility of a twelve- and eight-year-old, in comparison to that of a forty-year-old. Examples like these fly in the face of our private logic about our own neededness. We assume we are needed far beyond what is reasonable and that our kids are far less competent than they are. We're wrong on both counts.

If you're still in doubt, let's demonstrate the point with a few quick examples common to the experience of most parents. For example, you may have contracted the worst case of flu you've ever had in years and lost all capacity to "provide" for your family. You surface from your bedroom three days later to discover that your kids didn't starve! Not only that, they even managed to fix you a little something to eat from time to time.

Another case might be when you spend a week on vacation and leave your children with friends. You provide special cooking instructions for your youngest daughter's special needs and have gone so far as to provide an ample supply of select foods she is willing to eat. When you get home, your friends return all the chow you bought because your daughter ate as if she were at a smorgasboard the entire week. You wonder aloud, "How can this be?"

These last examples provide an invaluable lesson. Children usually expect parents to provide things for them because parents *do* provide things for them. When serendipitous opportunities present themselves, children seize the moment and behave in an independent, responsible, and competent manner. You may wonder why your children take advantage of you. The reason can be simply put: children take advantage of their advantages—they'd be foolish not to.

On an encouraging note, children will also take advantage of opportunities to overcome adversity—to handle it, to be resourceful and independent, and to be responsible beyond your best expectations.

Many more examples could be given, but providing further evidence probably wouldn't be any more persuasive. At this point you either make a leap of faith or recognize yourself in the examples provided.

If you're still not convinced, there is one last step that might help you to believe in your children. There are times when, for one reason or another, you're preoccupied with your thoughts and problems while in the midst of some routine household chore. Simultaneously, one of your children makes repeated unsuccessful bids for your attention. As you are about to come out of your stupor to serve the youngster, he does for himself exactly what he was asking you to do. Your spacey detachment allowed you to get a sneak preview of how easily children can accommodate themselves if you let them! These "out-of-body" experiences can be very instructive, and while the point is not to shut your children out, it *is* the epitome of encouragement to assume that "they can handle it." What you did unintentionally—ignore bids for attention and service—is exactly what you might try as a means of encouragement.

Guidelines for Encouragement

Attitudes and Techniques

1. Have faith in the child. Let the child know your belief: "You can handle it."

2. Separate the deed from the doer.

3. Recognize effort made. Notice contribution, not lack of perfection.

4. Spend time with the child.

Communication

1. Make "I" statements.

2. Stay on the current issue.

3. Make requests, not demands.

4. Seek meaning by reflecting content and emotion.

5. Give support.

6. Voice observations and don't pass judgment.

7. Disclose your emotions.

8. Seek alternatives.

Your best communication skill is your own humanity. Your emotional reaction to the message will tell you why the child is sending the message and your intellect will tell you what is being said. When in doubt about what to say, your best guideline is...listen!

Listening and communicating effectively are major parts of courageous parenting and necessary in order to parent effectively. However, beyond keeping the flow of communication open, a legitimate atmosphere of encouragement must prevail in the home. Although this concept is simple, it is often difficult for parents to be genuinely encouraging. Being an encouraging parent doesn't mean doing for the child; in fact it usually means the opposite.

Our children are a lifelong investment. They are our personal heritage. What parental epitaph would you write across your tombstone? "They were loving parents." "She produced a great citizen." "He always had time for kids." What do you hope for, or expect of, your children when they enter the world at eighteen? Perhaps that they will be good citizens, cooperative, responsible, compassionate, sensitive to others, honest, responsible, happy, self-directed, independent, capable of giving and receiving love—generally saint-like.

Ironically, to foster these lofty qualities we often chide, scold, and ridicule. It would be nice if there were a pill that we could take that would constantly remind us to be compassionate, empathetic, and understanding of our children and mates! But there is no pill. Furthermore, we rarely contemplate the temporary nature of our existence and the comparatively short time we have with our children until those we love move out of our lives.

The reality of the natural order is that children will move on to families of their own. Children aren't possessions; you can possess the relationship and its memory—never the child. You can also have faith in your children and encourage them. Be courageous—never do for your children what they can do for themselves.

76

6
LOGICAL CONSEQUENCES:
Alternatives to Punishment

Discipline is education; punishment is pain in-flicted for crimes. Parents have been confusing these two for decades.

—F.M.

Encouragement fosters cooperative behavior, but there are times when another component is a necessary part of the "educational" process. For example, if Bill is standing in the hallway dripping wet yelling for a towel, Mom could deal with him by saying, "Bill, I'm sure you can handle it." In this instance encouragement is necessary and sufficient. On the other hand, if Bill is tardy for school and needs a ride and a written excuse in order to avoid detention, his parents should not provide either. The logical consequence of Bill's irresponsibility is to serve his detention, walk to school, and live with the academic consequences. In the latter case Bill is entitled to have the opportunity to overcome adversity. Holding Bill responsible for his irresponsibility means arranging or allowing logical consequences to educate him.

In one very special way, discipline and encouragement ought to be similar—they both should include the opportunity to overcome adversity.

As children are encouraged to handle their own affairs or are disciplined by facing the logical consequences of their actions, they gain competence, self-esteem, and courage. Remember, as explained earlier, discipline is educational, punishment isn't. Discipline in its purest form provides moral, physical, and mental training. A concert pianist is disciplined. So is an Olympic athlete. Unfortunately, most parents punish instead of discipline. Discipline, after all, should provide children and adults with a clear sense of what ought to be done in a situation today and tomorrow; it is always future-oriented and instructional. Punishment doesn't meet either of these criteria. Punishment is neither future-oriented nor instructive. In fact, it focuses on the past and fails to provide opportunities for overcoming adversity—just opportunities to endure pain and discouragement.

ADVERSITY AND OPPORTUNITY

It is difficult to become committed to discipline as an educational process unless you are emotionally willing to give up old beliefs. Lack of commitment to change is stubbornly supported by erroneous notions about the "good old ways." However, most of us have forgotten what it was like to be on the receiving end of a punitive sentence. This lapse of memory is so pervasive one wonders whether senility and parenthood occur simultaneously.

For a moment consider an unpleasant episode you have had with an adult recently, one that left you feeling hurt or angry. Reflect on one of these experiences, and you might generate a situation very much like the one involving the woman below:

> My mother-in-law asked me to send out an announcement to our sorority stewardship committee concerning pledges. I agreed to take on the job and had drafted a document to be sent to the members of the committee. The letter was sitting on my desk waiting to be mailed last week, and my mother-in-law, who was visiting for supper, made a point of inspecting the letter. After dinner, she commented obliquely about the appropriateness of my approach. I told her my rationale for doing it the way I had, but she seemed unimpressed. The next morning my mother-in-law phoned and abruptly announced that I need not bother with the letter—she had seen to it and it was already mailed.

This ought to generate some of those old emotions you experienced when you were on the receiving end of punishment. Mom had suggested, autocratically, that the daughter-in-law take on this responsibility. The latter tackled the task only to have the mother-in-law autocratically critique her efforts. She was humiliated by the autocratic takeover and enraged by her sense of powerlessness. In a very critical way, the older woman's actions were contrary to what was socially appropriate and reasonable, and the daughter-in-law was furious. The very idea of the mother-in-law standing in judgment of something she was perfectly capable of doing was devastating. She vowed: 1) that she would get even; and 2) that she would never cooperate with her again. This was a punishing experience and it lends itself well to identifying the discouraging elements of punishment.

Characteristics of Punishment

1. Punishment is based upon a one up/one down or superior-to-inferior relationship.

2. No choices are provided for the child or opportunity for negotiation.

3. The adult assumes responsibility for the consequences of the child's actions.

4. The action taken (the punishment itself) does not relate logically to the misbehavior.

5. Punishment does not attempt to separate the deed from the doer, i.e., it does not make a distinction between the child being "bad" vs. the behavior being "bad." As a result, punishment is laden with moral injunctions about the child's worth.

6. The punishing action diminishes the dignity of both the parent and child; it also builds feelings of resentment in the child and a desire for retaliation.

FOUNDATIONS FOR LOGICAL CONSEQUENCES

As kids, we learned some of our best lessons when our surroundings or the family order were brought to bear upon us. Our actions and the consequences which followed were far more potent instruction than words or lectures. As a youngster, I grew up on the Mississippi and fished commercially. The river was often treacherous and deceptive.

After working years for the money to buy an outboard motor to replace my oars, I drove my new motor onto a rocky shallow and mutilated the propeller.

As I lifted the propeller out of the water, the voice of my uncle rang in my ears, "Always ride the high bank." I looked around and realized that I had driven obliviously along the low bank. I looked at the prop and knew it could only be replaced with a six-week catch. Putting the oars in the oarlocks, I started home with my uncle's refrain ringing in my ears, "Always ride the high bank." I never forgot it again! The prophecy had little impact until the river imprinted her lesson. From that day forward, I was attentive to banks and shallows and developed a firm respect for nature's consequences.

Many parents use natural consequences intuitively, knowing that natural consequences can be great educators. The most significant aspects of natural consequences are as follows:

1. The reality of the natural order affects the child directly.

2. The child is left responsible for his/her own condition.

3. The impact of the natural consequence may be, but need not be, painful, although any pain generated is a product of the child's own action and not the action of others.

4. The results have survival value and are logically related to the natural order.

Natural consequences are nature's educators. Failing to attend to the natural environment of the river led to financial calamity for me. The lesson learned was unfortunate and costly but not nearly as costly as it might have been. Had the prophecy been about river storms, I may have paid a greater price. The danger, of course, is that natural consequences may often be harmful and therefore cannot be relied on exclusively.

Life-threatening events generate the Mack-truck syndrome. Parents say, "Yeah sure, but if you let your kids play in the street, they'll get hit by a Mack truck!" That is exactly why we can't rely upon natural consequences as our sole means of discipline. However, parents must be able to set limits for their children without stripping them of responsibility. It's easy to recognize the value of natural consequences, and it's possible to apply these principles to most disciplinary or learning situations. By reviewing the positive components of natural consequences and the negative aspects of punishment, we have the foundation for positive disciplinary alternatives—logical consequences.

LOGICAL CONSEQUENCES OR EDUCATIONAL DISCIPLINE

A logical consequence is no more than a natural consequence extended to include the limits of family, time, and the larger community (social order). A citizen may choose to run a red light and risk being broadsided by the "Mack truck." The risk is particularly great if the intersection is blind. To prevent accidents society has established the following logical consequence: if you run a red light, you will get a ticket and be liable for a fine.

However, there aren't many logical consequences established by society for a child who is irresponsible, disobedient, or rude. Therefore, parents have to try to find, or manufacture, discipline; they have to find strategies that will train and educate the child quickly. These logical consequences are alternatives arranged for a child by an adult, or negotiated between the child and the adult. The alternatives offered require a decision by the child and are designed to have the child assume maximum responsibility for his/her actions. The outcome of the child's choice—the consequence—dramatizes the result of cooperative vs. uncooperative behavior.

For a child who is rude, a logical consequence arranged by the parent might be this: "If you're going to be rude, we're not going to listen. You may go to your room." When the child chooses to be polite, s/he stays in the living area with the rest of the family. If not, s/he must go (or be removed) to his/her room.

A logical consequence which is negotiated between the parent(s) and child might go something like this:

Child: Mom/Dad, I want to take piano lessons.

Parent: I'm glad you're interested in music. However, you're already taking guitar lessons. Do you think you'll have time to practice both?

Child: Yes, if I alternate days with each instrument.

Parent: Okay, but it's still a big commitment of your time and our money. How about this—we'll pay as long as you keep up your practice schedule. But if you don't practice, you'll have to pay for the piano lessons out of your allowance. Is that a deal?

Child: It's a deal.

Many more examples could be given, but in general parents can create logical consequences providing educational discipline for their children by following the guidelines listed below.

Guidelines for Creating Logical Consequences

1. Assume that children and adults are of equal dignity and worth, but not equal ability.

2. Use actions and not words.

3. Provide choices that are logically related to the misbehavior and the limits of the family and larger community (i.e., recognize the social context of behavior).

4. Maintain an attitude of firmness and fairness, where firmness proclaims your (adult) need for dignity and fairness expresses the child's need for the same.

5. Negotiate alternatives in advance whenever possible, maintaining a calm atmosphere, not angry or hurtful.

If we follow these principles in our efforts to discipline or "educate" our children, we're likely to have the impact that Scottish statesman Lord Brougham suggested: "Education makes people easy to lead but difficult to drive, easy to govern but impossible to enslave."

THE FAMILY PIT

But how do you turn the guidelines above into concrete action? The remainder of the book will be devoted to specific examples, but for immediate demonstration let's consider a typical hassle. Children's toys often find their way into all corners of the house without ever being returned to their proper places. With all the wisdom and guile we can muster, we attack the family pit in one of several ways. We try our favorite lecture; and while we may like it, it falls upon deaf ears and we fall over the toys.

Sometimes we try threats, "If you don't pick these up, you're going to your room for the night." Since it's 9:00 P.M., children think it's a great idea and retire happily. Finally we stoop to the lowest of adult behavior and say, "I'm throwing away everything on the floor you don't pick up." The next day you discover your wallet and glasses in the trash compactor.

You can develop logical consequences instead of counter-productive threats by applying the five principles above. At a neutral time, not during the heat of battle, ask the youngster if s/he is tired of your constant nagging about toys. Empathize with the child's annoyance and make a commitment to stop. Acknowledge the youngster's ability to handle the situation and act as if s/he can handle it, whether you believe it or not! Voice your concerns about the unfairness involved for both of you. (Nagging is unfair to the kids because it belittles them, and it's unfair to you because you always have the responsibility of picking up.) Then, suggest the "mystery box" as a solution.

The mystery box involves choices. Get a large box into which all possessions will go if left lying about the house. The choice is this—the youngsters may pick up their toys or you will. Say nothing, but take action. If the belongings aren't picked up each evening by a certain time, you'll pick up. The choice is theirs. If you pick up, belongings go in the mystery box. The mystery is where the box is and when they get their toys back! Critical to the mystery box is the mystery. The box must not become a Saturday box or a good behavior box. Toys are returned only when the youngsters demonstrate their cooperation by picking up their toys in a responsible manner. You will know this has happened when you go around the house in the evening and there is nothing to pick up.

The mystery box is usually effective because it adheres to the principles of logical consequences cited earlier: 1) the solution is negotiated, not dictated; 2) parent and child both have dignity; 3) youngsters are provided with choices; 4) action steps are taken instead of talking and blaming; 5) the atmosphere is friendly and civil; 6) youngsters assume responsibility for their toys.

The mystery box is most effective when parents negotiate the terms of the box with children. If you see the "box" technique as a cleverly camouflaged means of winning, your children will feel betrayed and act accordingly. To avoid this pitfall, talk about what will be picked up and by whom. Since the principles apply equally, if Dad is in the habit of leaving his coat on the chair in the hall and the family decides that all coats will be hung up, you'll have to negotiate what is to be done. If you act arbitrarily, the kids will misinterpret your intentions and react vindictively. (When dealing with adolescents, it's better to have a "central location box" because they generally react negatively to terms used for younger children, like the "mystery box.")

Logical consequences are a package deal, not merely techniques. Like encouragement, they imply an attitude that goes far beyond any technique. Most disciplinary situations lend themselves to logical consequences, but the foundation must be laid carefully. Logical consequences are extremely potent interventions and can easily be misinterpreted by children. If parents fail to serve notice at a neutral time, kids will inevitably interpret them as unfair and hurtful. By serving notice, however, these difficulties are minimized, or as Ralph Waldo Emerson said, "The secret of education lies in 'respecting' the pupil."

Any potent intervention strategy can be misused and misinterpreted, and some cautions are necessary. Logical consequences can be felt to be punitive if the principles and guidelines are misinterpreted.

USING LOGICAL CONSEQUENCES TO DERAIL MISBEHAVIOR

In order to use logical consequences effectively there are seven major principles to understand and then apply.

1. *Identify the child's useless goal.* As we indicated in chapter three, children pursue the four goals (attention-getting, bids for power, revenge and counter-hurt, and assumed disability) rather exclusively and know what their payoffs are. Implementing logical consequences requires recognition and understanding of these emotional goals. In order to recognize the useless goals of children, it helps to have a certain "out-of-body" detachment, a distancing of self from the impact of the child's actions. In clinical situations, I have occasionally videotaped transactions among family members and replayed them at a later date. Watching the replay gives parents and kids the distance necessary to view their actions objectively.

If you don't have the benefit of videotape or an impartial observer, watch the actions of your children as they make demands or pester you. Watch for a minute, don't listen! Watch the child's facial expressions, body language and gestures, but don't listen to the language. In other words, act as if you're outside the situation. This self-imposed distancing will amplify the child's misdirected behavior.

For example, several years ago a friend of mine was waiting in line to cash a check at a bank. His youngest son, age four, began whining for some gum from a gumball machine which was located at the cashier's window. Dad tried to ignore his son's snivelling but it grew worse. Finally, Junior threw himself on the floor in a thrashing rage. As soon as the boy's head hit the floor, Dad headed for the door. Junior was so busy thrashing he didn't see Dad leave. Suddenly, Junior opened his eyes and realized Dad was gone. He stopped crying immediately and his eyes darted quickly about searching for his father. Realizing Dad was indeed gone, he scrambled quickly to his feet, jammed his hands into his pockets and walked nonchalantly toward the door as if to say to bystanders, "You didn't really see me do that!"

If you observe the behaviors employed by your children, such as temper, tears, or attention-getting, you quickly realize how purposeful they are. Most importantly, you'll understand that these emotions are directed at, and intended for, you—and you alone.

To derail children's misbehavior in one of the four categories, logical consequences can be used as follows:

(a) *Attention-getting*—Attention-getting mechanisms demand attention or service. Therefore, logical consequences should avoid providing service or attention, thus effectively disciplining the child.

(b) *Bids for Power*—Power struggles often require consequences, but these consequences may be perceived by the child as punitive. In the case of power then, parents must serve notice in advance of their change in discipline strategy and negotiate the alternatives with the child. If you have become accustomed to arbitrary decision-making, you're probably reluctant to accept negotiation. But think for a moment about the last time your spouse told (rather than *asked*) you to do something for him or her that was equally inconvenient for you. You probably railed at the presumptuousness. When adults fail to serve notice, children react with the same sense of indignity, the same sense of disqualification and discouragement. So, when generating logical consequences, be sure that the actions you take are designed to control the *situation*—not the child.

(c) *Revenge and Counter-hurt*—In most families, vengeful behavior is minor or infrequent, but when this behavior becomes the rule rather than the exception, the child has become deeply discouraged. In these cases the family ought to feel free to seek professional help. Because continuously vengeful kids are deeply discouraged, it's difficult for them to differentiate between punishing ultimatums and legitimate choices. If you have a vengeful child, the change in strategy won't be easy. If you want things to change, then your parenting options seem to be encouragement and *natural* consequences. Natural consequences are those imposed by civil authority or the natural order, not parental authority, and so are most appropriate when vengeful behaviors include stealing, bullying, driving while intoxicated, etc. You can't prevent or shelter the child from the civil consequences of these actions. Trying to protect children from civil authority is like clinging to the myths that parents know and control all, acting as if you can usurp the legal system.

When parents place themselves in the role of Supreme Court justices, it has a paradoxical effect. Children will likely continue to misbehave, believing that their parents are the final authority. But, if parents serve notice to children that they will have to live with the natural and perhaps legal consequences of their actions, then children may become more responsible.

As an adolescent, when I left the house on Saturday night, my father would say with a wry, but serious grin, "If you get thrown in jail I'll bring you beer and cigarettes." Since I was capable of real mischief but didn't smoke cigarettes or drink much, I got the message—"You're responsible for your actions. I won't bail you out!"

Acts of revenge are beyond the scope of logical consequences. In these instances, rely exclusively upon natural consequences and encouragement. The vengeful child will find it difficult or impossible to accept logical consequences from adults without vengeance. These youngsters feel so hurt that when adults establish logical consequences, the kids feel they've been punished. Hence, it is imperative that vengeful kids are able to separate your actions and the actions of other adults from the consequences of their behavior.

(d) *Assumed disability*—When a child's pattern of behavior is to assume disability, then s/he is deeply discouraged. (Occasional instances of assumed disability may occur for many children, however, just as the "normal" child is sometimes vengeful.) But instead of striking out at others as the vengeful child does, s/he withdraws. This child's discouragement is so complete that s/he believes it's easier to give up than it is to try and fail. Our emotional need to rescue the child far exceeds the child's need to be rescued. Contrary to what we might expect, the child who assumes a disability may benefit from logical consequences. In this case, particularly, the opportunity to overcome adversity can be very encouraging, because once the child meets the challenge, s/he is no longer disabled. Of greatest importance, however, is the child's *need* for encouragement. The automatic guideline in these cases is—don't give up and don't pity.

2. *Be sure that the consequence is, in fact, an opportunity to overcome adversity and not arbitrary punishment.* A consequence need not hurt to be instructive. Sometimes parents give up on consequences because they see no evidence of pain: "If it isn't hurting the child, it can't be working." This rationale may be tied to their own need to subordinate the child.

An effective consequence ought to be instructive and achievable, not a pain threshold test. In some instances, overcoming adversity will be painful but it need not be. Children ought to learn to be cooperative because it is useful, not because it hurts.

3. *A consequence should focus on the adult gaining control of the situation, not the child.* Adults who use consequences to control the child will discover that children quickly diagnose the manipulation and sabotage the strategy.

4. *Discuss alternatives at a neutral time.* If you fail to do this, the child will feel ambushed and the logical consequence may backfire into revenge. Obviously, it is not always possible to negotiate alternatives for misbehavior in advance, but in the heat of battle you can always agree to stop fighting and negotiate at a later time.

5. *Once choices have been made, stop talking and act.* At times consequences appear rather severe from the adult's perspective. At this point, you want to absorb the blow for the child. The end result is debilitating. When a consequence is available, reasonable, and instructive, allow it to take its course. Remember, children base their actions upon your actions, not your words.

6. *Identify who owns the problem.* There are generally three possibilities: 1) the child owns it; 2) the adult owns it; 3) the adult and child own it. In the first instance, logical consequences are not required because natural conquences will provide all the instruction necessary.

In the second and third cases, logical consequences can usually be used to resolve the situation. A brief example of each may be helpful.

(a) The child owns the problem: Sue is late for school, hasn't cleaned her room, and is unable to find her books. It's clear the situation is neither the adult's doing nor responsibility. Although the girl may be late for school, that ought to be between the youngster and the school; it is not a time for a parent to bail out the child by driving her so she's on time. Many parents put themselves in the child's shoes and worry about the embarrassment it would cause, but the emphasis should be on what the child needs to learn and less about how s/he would feel. Parents tend to make a leap of logic once they understand what the consequences are. First they decide the consequences will produce bone-crushing humiliation (false) and then they decide that the child can't handle it (also false). Once parents believe in the child's competence, allowing the logical consequence to educate the child will become easier.

(b) The adult owns the problem: Sue has taken tools from her father's workbench and has failed to return them. Clearly, the child's actions are causing difficulty for Dad. Limits must be set to protect his rights as well as the child's. This point is often ignored. We mistakenly assume that by respecting the child's rights, we must relinquish our own to the arbitrary whims of the child. The reverse is also true. Adults expect children to relinquish their rights to their spontaneous adult demands. Both of these assumptions are based upon self-centered thinking.

When one family member's behavior infringes upon the rights, opportunity, or safety of another, a consequence is required. If tools are lost, Sue must be held financially responsible. If the episode repeats itself, all tools will have to be placed under lock and key and Sue and her siblings will have to forfeit access to them.

(c) The adult and child own the problem: Dad has his heart set on watching the evening news, the children are determined to watch "Sesame Street," and the programs air simultaneously. In this instance, there is joint ownership of the problem. Therefore, discipline isn't required, negotiation is. Applying logical consequences in such cases may be a sophisticated way of gaining arbitrary compliance to adult demands. Children quickly recognize the differences between authentic choice and arbitrary demands. Adolescents and most younger children know immediately whether parents intend to negotiate or manipulate.

On the other hand, if the consequences which are negotiated are agreeable to adults as well as kids, they may be extremely useful in the situation.

7. *Withdraw from power struggles and conflict.* Don't give in and don't give up. In other words, "take your sails out of their wind." The child may be too emotional to reason; then it becomes the adult's responsibility to defuse the situation. Again the guideline is, seek to control yourself and the situation, not the child. If you look carefully at your actions and those of your children, you will see that your child is not controlled by you, but controls him/her self. Control is an illusion maintained by two people.

F.A.C.E.N.

It's hard to remember all the guidelines for applying logical consequences. Try this acronym as a reminder, F.A.C.E.N. Try thinking in terms of "facen" responsibilities. This is a short list of the most essential elements:

1. F—Remain *firm* and *fair*.

2. A—*Act*, don't talk.

3. C—Provide *choices* that relate to the misbehavior and the order of the family, time, and the larger community.

4. E—Assume that you and the child are of *equal* dignity and worth, but not ability.

5. N—*Negotiate* choices and consequences with children at neutral times and in advance of misbehavior as much as possible.

Summary

These disciplinary strategies are only as strong as your commitment to be an encouraging parent. Regardless of your theoretical orientation or technique, the effects of discipline are short-lived if the child doesn't feel encouraged. Natural and logical consequences capitalize on the instructions of nature, time, family limits, and the community; and these are congruent with our system of government and life in a democracy in general. If a person's worth is ultimately measured by his/her contribution, logical consequences are the most reasonable, purest means of disciplining and educating children.

Although powerful educators by themselves, logical consequences can be augmented by demonstrating to kids that encouraging cooperative behavior works. Parents can model the power of cooperative behavior by giving up the swagger stick and the ghost of control. Then they can lead by example.

PART THREE

SOLVING PROBLEMS
FOR ALL AGES

7
MAKING TIME SPECIAL
FOR YOU AND YOUR KIDS

There is no conventional structure for nuclear-family-behavior-during-blizzards, so we face one another with delight and surprise. Dozens of times I've heard [families] say, "We did whatever we liked; we talked a lot."

—*Carol Bly*
Letters from the Country

WHAT SPECIAL TIME ISN'T

Parents often say, "Oh, yeah, I spend time with the kids on Wednesday evenings after dinner—*if* I'm home." Or, "I usually take him/her down to the ball game *if* our team is having a good season." Or, "That all depends on my schedule. We do something together on weekends *if* I'm not too swamped." This is an "iffy" business.

Spending time with the children is one of the most valuable things parents can do. Yet, much of the value is lost if the time is arbitrarily determined by the parent for his or her convenience and interest. Typically the adult dictates when and where time will be spent, and the child doesn't have much to say about it. In the eyes of the child, this makes a tremendous difference. When the child does have a say in the matter, special time spent together builds a sense of trust, equality, and commitment.

WHAT IS SPECIAL TIME?

Making time for children means exactly that. Usually we try to find time. We make (or set aside) time for everything else, but try to find it (use extra time as it becomes available) for our kids. For most of us, that free time is only found alongside the pot of gold at the end of the rainbow—and the relationship with our children suffers as a result. Special time is a block of prearranged time designated as the child's time with you—one child plus one parent. It's the child's time! The child determines what to do, when to do it, and whether to do it at all.

With adolescents the latter is often an issue. When approached with the notion of special time together older kids may initially spurn the idea as "dumb." If you have teenagers, there's no need to give special time a special name—don't call it anything! "Special" time is an attractive label to young children, but teenagers will probably laugh you out of the house. Nevertheless, even these older kids will think driving practice, or lunch at a special place would be fun, or that an afternoon at the river, shore, ballpark, or symphony would be a neat change of pace. Soon children of all ages come to value the time spent with their parents as much as the activity.

Special time is an intimate frame in a day, set aside for parent and child encouragement. You are unconditionally available to the child regardless of the youngster's conduct throughout the day. It's your opportunity to teach the child that s/he is good enough just as he or she is. However, you aren't obligated to chase down the kid in order to have special time; you're just obligated to offer, not guarantee that it happens. Nor do you have to comply with an unreasonable demand. If the child asks you to go two miles across town to an ice cream store and return with a sundae, forget it. On the other hand, if the child asks you to accompany him or her to an ice cream store for a favorite sundae, it's a reasonable request so long as the parent is willing to spend the money or the child is willing to treat.

Steps for Implementing Special Time

1. Introduce the concept of special time to the child.

At a neutral time, ask the child if s/he would be interested in spending special time with you every other day, week, etc.

Your approach has to be different with adolescents. You may have to ask for time with them because "you" need it. If necessary, assure them that their friends won't see them. But the child should understand that it will be his or her own time with you, to do as he or she wishes within the limits of mutual respect and physical reality.

2. *Negotiate a time with the child.*

Discuss appropriate and convenient times with the child, stipulating when you can meet regularly and, in turn, ask the child to select a preferred time. The amount of time spent with the child is an individual matter which might vary from the weekday to the weekend. The guide to action should be your ability to fulfill the commitment.

3. *Adhere to the schedule.*

Once a time has been established, it is helpful to post the schedule in a central location. When families first try special time, they frequently cancel, skip, or inadvertently miss it. A schedule helps both parents and children remember. When it is necessary to reschedule a session, it should be negotiated democratically.

4. *Special time is offered unconditionally.*

This time is offered unconditionally regardless of the child's conduct throughout the course of the day. It is designed to teach the child, via deed and word, that he or she is a valued individual. There is one exception to this rule, however. If the child is uncooperative, destructive, or disrespectful to you during the special time, you are not obligated to continue. You can cancel the session until the next time, or stop temporarily and resume the activity when the child chooses to cooperate.

5. *Special time is for one child and parent.*

Unless otherwise negotiated, special time is designed for one parent and child. It is that particular child's time with the parent of his or her choice, as long as arrangements are made with each child and parent. Parents of large families may have to alternate children every other week.

6. *The child has freedom of choice.*

The child has the freedom to choose the activity within reasonable limits of parental time, financial resources, and individual rights. (That means you as a parent should not sacrifice your own rights or dignity.) With younger children, you may have to offer a series of activities from which the child may choose. You may suggest Legos, reading *The Rescuers*, or sledding for half an hour. The child can then choose among these activities.

For adolescents you probably won't have to generate options. A favorite for them is going out for a little driving practice or shopping. Some of the best opportunities to talk are provided when both of you are captive in the car without the possibility of interruption.

Typical activities chosen by children include lunch, shopping, sledding, reading, bicycle riding, fixing something, cleaning something, building something, or going to a movie, play, symphony, library or sporting event.

WHAT CAN BE ACCOMPLISHED?

Special time can serve many useful purposes and eliminate many conflicts. If your son is demanding you play a certain game, you can refuse the bid for attention by saying, "I would like to play, but I must finish reading this book. I would be glad to play with you during special time if you like."

In struggles for power, the strategy is not as direct but equally effective. During special time—let's say it's with your daughter this time—you say via word and deed, "You are the boss; I am here to do as you choose as long as you respect my rights and dignity." You comply with her requests and suggestions, acknowledging her rights in the situation. Further, by respecting your daughter's decision, you tell her that her ideas and capabilities are valuable and to be seriously considered.

Because you take action on the word of the child, she experiences cooperative, democratic action firsthand. If she decides to work with plastic shrink art and in the process asks you to help, the tables are turned. Now you respond to requests and help accomplish a task. Then she can recognize the cooperation and respect that you are offering.

By example, the child experiences the benefits and good feelings of cooperative behavior and comes to value it.

Because you attend exclusively to the child and stay in close physical contact, there are always opportunities for encouragement. Give yourself unconditionally to the child, whether it's a son or daughter, even if it's only for a short time.

You and your child will both experience satisfaction, warmth, and self-esteem. Instead of feeling guilty about not "finding" time for your children, make it. Dreikurs said that "guilt is just a means of calling attention to the good intentions we never had." Actions speak louder than words, hence the importance of special time. You will feel effective and fulfilled and so will your children.

A FINAL NOTE

There is a direct, inverse relationship between misbehavior and special time: as the latter increases the former decreases. You may be surprised to find that children of all ages value the occasion whether it's called cruising, lunch, or has no special name at all. This time models democratic behavior and offers conclusive evidence that cooperation is not philosophical pie in the sky, but encouragement at its best.

8

GIVING UP THE SWAGGER STICK AND THE GHOST OF CONTROL: Family Council

The ideal aim of education is creation of the power of self-control.

—John Dewey

TRAINING GROUND FOR DECISION-MAKING

"At your age when my father said jump, I asked how high on the way up." How many times have you said something tired and trivial like this? Archie Bunker couldn't have put it better himself. We try desperately to command authority or cajole respect from our kids, but a statement like "When I was your age..." is the kiss of death. Kids can't imagine a fossil like you was ever their age, and they're stone deaf before you finish the sentence. You don't command respect by talking about how respectful you were as a child—only by being worthy of respect as an adult! Any old Marine will tell you that leadership, or true authority, is achieved by winning the respect, cooperation, and trust of others by example. You can't talk the game unless you're willing to play it.

FAMILY COUNCIL

The family council will give your family a chance to generate cooperative leadership. Parents are often apprehensive about sharing power or control with their children, but if you look carefully, you'll discover that your kids already have a way of doing just about what they want to do. Parents simply live with the ghost of control, the fiction—not the reality.

The more rigidly you hold to your illusion, the less leadership you will provide. Strength and force are two very different things. You exercise strength when you realize power must be shared by everyone. You exert force when you cling to the fictitious notion that you're the "boss" and all kids need to do is check in with you for further orders. Your kids are the toughest troops you'll ever have to lead, and that's exactly what you must do—lead. The first step is to give up the swagger stick of authority and the ghost of control. Next, to lead your family, you must provide a structure that truly models cooperative, democratic living skills. One such structure or technique is the family council. During the family council meetings children are asked to take a legitimate and responsible part in family decision-making.

Introducing the Idea

How is this council supposed to work? What gets discussed? How do you maintain order? What business is appropriate for these meetings? The following is a slightly edited script from one family's meeting.

Kristin, age 11, calls the meeting to order, "Secretary please read the minutes of the last meeting." Lettie, age 7, proceeds to read the minutes. Kristin then moves to old business..."Jobs. Since I'm the chair I get first pick of jobs, then the secretary (Lettie), and then the chart person (Mom) and then Dad." Each member makes his or her selection in turn until all of the jobs have been accounted for.

Kristin: Any other old business? The chair recognizes Mom.
Mom: Now that I am working full time I am having to do too many chores around the house. I was willing to do more when I wasn't working, but it's different now.
Lettie: I am doing all of my jobs!
Mom: I know you are doing all of your jobs and I appreciate it very much, but that's not the issue exactly.
Kristin: Mother, I feel like Lettie does, so if we're going to decide anything maybe you better tell us exactly what it is you don't want to do.
Mom: Well, I am satisfied with our cooking arrangements, where I cook three meals a week and you split the rest, so that's okay,

but I am tired of trying to get everyone to pick their clothes up in their rooms and in the hall.

Kristin: Okay, clothes. Anything else?

Mom: Well, yes—music lessons.

Kristin: Music lessons? I don't see how that's connected!

Mom: Well, my work schedule is exhausting and I can't supervise your voice lessons as well as Lettie's cello.

Kristin: Okay, music and clothes. Anything else?

Mom: No.

Kristin: How do the rest of you feel about these two things?

Dad: Well, Mom has a point. Without her income we wouldn't be able to have a lot of the things we do, so it's important to all of us that she work, but it isn't fair to her to have to work two jobs. I think it will be hard to work out a solution for both of these things tonight. Which is most important to you?

Mom: Both are equally tiring but I would be willing to talk about lessons next week.

Kristin: Okay. Let's talk about clothes and rooms. I am tired of having Mom and Dad nag me about my dirty clothes in my room.

Lettie: Yea. It would be a lot easier for me to keep my room clean if Mom didn't bug me about my clothes all the time. It would be easier for me to keep my room clean if I did my own wash!

Dad: You're telling us it would be easier for you to do one job by taking on two more? I don't know.

Kristin: I agree with Lettie, I'd rather do my own wash than worry about you and Mom always bugging us about it.

Mom: Can the two of you handle it?

Kristin: Mom, when Aunt Joan was sick last summer we did all the wash for two weeks by ourselves. Dad barely helped.

Dad: Wait a minute, I hear about four loads of wash going a day. That would get expensive. Why can't we just rotate jobs as washer person like we do a lot of the other jobs?

Kristin: No, that would mean all of us would still have to run by one schedule and that's unfair and too hard to coordinate.

Lettie: My problem is everyone telling me what to do. I'd be better off alone.

Mom: The extra expense would be worth it to me as long as we weren't being wasteful.

Lettie: How about if you don't have ten items you can't run a load?

Kristin: Five.

Dad: I can't agree with that. Our water bill would skyrocket.

Mom: Well, I think ten items is sufficient. There are many nights when I run a load of shirts for Dad and there are less than ten shirts in the machine.

Dad: Sounds as if the three of you have an agreement. I'll go along with it for awhile, but if it isn't working we get to try it my way after a week. Agreed?

Kristin: Other old business...

Getting Started

Such are the workings of a family council. The vignette is a true script of a negotiation from one family's meeting. And, at last report, the agreement was working well. Not surprisingly, these little girls weren't little at all in terms of their capabilities. Lettie and Kristin demonstrated their competence in spite of their parent's initial opposition.

The family in question flowed through their negotiation with suspicious ease, but that's probably because they have been conducting their business in this manner for several years.

Things don't always run that smoothly in the beginning. Yet, with hard work and encouragement, the process soon pays off. The earlier you start family councils, the easier and more effective they will be. But the process will work even if you start when your children are adolescents provided you hang in there.

Introduce the notion of a family council at a neutral time. Simply say that you have some ideas about changing the way decisions are made in the family, but you need their (the children's) help. Ask them what they think about having family meetings or councils in which major family decisions would be made. These decisions could involve any or all of the following: vacations, outings, discipline, special times, etc. Present an honest assessment of the impact you expect the children to have on major decisions. Recognize that there are certain decisions over which no one will have control. Job transfers, for instance, may fall in this category, but within these constraints the family may begin to share far more of the decision-making process. Be careful to focus on the positive aspects of family meetings, avoiding the appearance—or reality—of the meeting as a disciplinary session.

102

Guidelines for Getting Started

1. Find a structured, but relaxed place to hold the meeting where all the family members can be alert, yet comfortable. Encourage everyone living in the household to attend, toddlers and grandparents, everyone.

2. Keep a formal record. This requires a secretary, and this responsibility as well as that of the chairperson should rotate to include the youngest family members capable of participating. The secretarial responsibilities should be modeled and shared in such a way as to discourage sex-role stereotyping. Surprisingly, even very young children can serve as the secretary by recording the events that transpire, by drawing pictures or by using a tape recorder. In the beginning the leadership role should be held by someone other than the traditional person. If Dad has been the authority figure, someone else, perhaps Mom or an older sister, should serve as the first chairperson.

3. When generating guidelines to facilitate discussion, avoid arbitrary rules. Encourage family members to establish the guidelines needed to conduct the family business. Parents can get things started by asking questions like: How long should we meet? How will we insure that everyone gets an opportunity to talk? How long will we be able to talk about an issue? What things can we talk about? These leads will elicit input from everyone. During the first meetings parents can suggest agendas. A typical agenda might include some of the items below:
   a. Reading the minutes of previous meeting.
   b. Calendar for the coming week.
   c. Banking and other financial matters.
   d. Family fun time.
   e. Old business (jobs).
   f. New business.
   g. "The nicest thing that happened to me this week" spot.
   h. Wrap up and family game or family special time.

Agendas for future meetings can be generated by keeping a piece of paper in a convenient place—on the refrigerator, for example. As people walk by and think of things, they can scribble them on the list. In this way the agenda items generated reflect the concerns of everyone—all family members, not just Mom and Dad.

4. Make the meeting a pleasant and encouraging experience. Focus on the positive and allow the kids to voice their views. When issues reach a decision point, try to reach consensus; avoid bringing things to a vote. This may seem strange at first, but there is a good reason to avoid voting. Voting polarizes the minority, however small, and they can easily sabotage the efforts of the rest of the family. Trying to achieve consensus is far better. If a minority prefers A to B, ask them if they would be willing to try A for a week. At the end of that time everyone will try B. If you reach an impasse, you can decide not to decide.

GETTING THE JOB DONE

I have used family meetings on a regular basis with children from the age of four to eighteen, in adolescent group homes and in my own family. I have had cross-generational meetings which included grandparents and children and to the amazement of all of us, they work.

In group homes for adolescent offenders, youth from all backgrounds, including minority and ghetto children, assumed responsibility beautifully. While working in group home settings I found the family meeting became a focal point of the treatment process. Group decisions made by youth included establishing monthly menus, determining group home outings, generating discipline, maintaining house rules, as well as other significant tasks. Family meetings within group homes have solved conflicts involving theft, sexual harassment, and death of a natural parent. In many of these group home meetings the children responsible for making the decision and generating the alternatives were court-referred or delinquent children. In the case of the death of a natural parent, the group generated a compassionate, mature response to the situation and made substantial contributions to the family. Some of my most creative ideas haven't been mine at all, but ideas generated by so-called "delinquents" at their family meetings.

Group home teenagers thought of using an egg timer as a means of controlling the time allowed each speaker. One court-referred youth suggested that any vandalism in the group home become the property and responsibility of the person responsible for the destruction, or the property of everyone living in the home. "You break it, you own it! If we can't determine who broke it, we all own it." These same young people decided that house parents were entitled to inspect every room in the home unannounced as long as pot smoking continued in the home and no one confronted the violators.

YOUR FAMILY AND MINE

Several years ago at one of our family meetings, the morning routine and getting up were the major topics of discussion. Our kindergartner decided that she no longer wanted our nagging advice during reveille. She wanted, and got, her own alarm clock. We were obviously pleased.

Things went along fine until the morning following Christmas break. We woke late to discover the house empty. Buffie had disappeared. There was no evidence of her anywhere. We dressed hurriedly and then contemplated our next move. Had she gone to school?

We dashed off to the elementary school, sheepishly slipped into the side door, and quietly peeked into the classroom. There she was. Grateful, we exited the building briskly, hoping not to be noticed. While both of us overslept, Buffie got herself up, ate, and left for school twenty minutes ahead of schedule.

At a family meeting we had decided anyone who was late in the morning would be left to experience the natural consequences of being tardy to work or school. In the first real test, Mom and Dad turned out to be negligent and the six-year-old proved responsible to Mom and Dad's embarrassment and the entertainment of the teacher. Buffie's reaction was, "I guess you decided to be late for work because you didn't need the money, huh?"

Young children realize quickly that something significant happens at family meetings. Soon they seek to be included, "I want a job too." They want to exercise the responsibility big sister or Dad has.

Once a four-year-old was listening to an exchange about TV scheduling in the family and raised her hand to make an announcement. "I know what cooperation is! Cooperation is having two TVs." Then she made an astute observation—that a second TV was too costly. We suggested she think about how to raise money to buy a second set. Amazingly, this four-year-old suggested charging a fee when family members watched commercial stations, while allowing educational

105

television to be free of charge. The suggestion was acted upon and a jar for the "family fun fund" was placed on the TV set; all who chose to watch commercial TV paid an hourly fee. Not surprisingly, the adults' viewing habits changed most dramatically. Paradoxically, once the fund was raised the family decided to stick with one TV and spend the fun fund on something else.

Insuring the integrity of family meetings is vital to their success. That means the adults must be certain that the meeting doesn't become a forum for parental soap-box speeches or discipline. Meetings should end on an upbeat note; a brief family game or treat can end the meeting pleasantly.

Further, meetings shouldn't become the focal point for problems and chores. To insure that positive things happen, limit the amount of time spent on various topics. Place jobs and discipline in the early part of the schedule to insure movement through these troublesome issues. Parents don't always know best. Oftentimes what could have easily been a battle of wills can become a well-negotiated compromise. A child is naturally inclined to cooperate unless badgered or humiliated by an adult.

Success depends heavily upon consistency and follow-through. Children will be naturally suspicious on both counts, and rightfully so. Meetings should be held every week. Consequences generated during the meeting must have time to have an effect on family members. And, the social order can become the driving force for change instead of the arbitrary power of the adult or whims of a child.

CHORES

If parents see the council as a new way to gain subtle control, then it is doomed. Similarly, if parents use the meeting to pass jobs out autocratically, the meetings will fail. Ask the kids for a list of things they believe need to be done in order for the home to run smoothly. Then, ask them to submit a list of jobs they feel competent to handle. Finally, establish a democratic way to dispense jobs. Some families decide to have family members choose with first choice going to the chairperson, since the chair shifts systematically from week to week. Others use a lottery. In any event, jobs should not be distributed autocratically by the parents.

For example, one family placed cleaning the truck on the family jobs list. Initially there was no problem, then hunting season opened. At the next family meeting the eldest daughter, age ten, observed that the truck was a mess from hunting trips and that it didn't seem fair to have to clean the truck if you didn't hunt. The rationale was undisputed. The job was removed from the list and became Dad's until hunting season was over.

Equal distribution of dignity and worth are dispensed during family meetings as these episodes illustrate, but the meeting is never intended to distribute ability or responsibility exactly the same to everyone. Indeed, treating people equally means treating them differently. Being democratic means people are entitled to equal dignity and worth, not that all people are of equal ability, skill or knowledge. The latter is patently false, but the former is a worthy goal which we pursue as a nation.

SEEING THE LIGHT

Parents benefit from family meetings in many ways. They learn about their children's interests and skills and often develop new interests of their own. Parents have been known to take up rock climbing, backpacking, photography, cycling, white water kayaking and even hang-gliding as a result of family outings planned. Children in some of these same families have taken up the adults' interests: cross country skiing, painting, pottery, hunting, fishing, and choir. During a family meeting one mother who knew nothing about gymnastics was asked by her daughter to be a gymnastics judge. This launched an entirely new interest and eventually a part-time job.

It is difficult to overemphasize the importance of family meetings. If meetings are implemented, chores and family routines become enjoyable. If scheduling is hit-and-miss, that's the way chores are done. There is no guarantee for success, but one thing can help: rather than having an adult ride herd on tasks, the agreements generated at the meeting can be monitored by checklists for each person. Throughout the week as chores and responsibilities are completed, they can be checked off by the person who did them. This system reinforces the feeling of accomplishment and encourages the individual to be responsible for his/her own behavior.

107

As families develop a routine, they discover their own innovations. However, with adolescents parents must be willing to live with marginal success during the early stages. Teenagers are suspicious of any effort to structure their lives and may see these meetings as a clandestine means of control.

Once family meetings are established, you'll feel that they are a necessity, not a gimmick. The family council is more than a problem-solving technique—it's group encouragement for each member and for the family unit as a whole.

9
REVERSE PUPPETS
AND OTHER REBELS

*Once parents experience their inability to control
the lives of others, they are a step closer to controlling their own lives.*

—*F. M.*

REVERSE PUPPETS

Everyone has known a James Dean reincarnated—someone who isn't
happy unless he is suffering as a result of his own stubborn opposition
to everything. Some people only know what they're against but not
what they're for. Rebels know only that which they oppose. Yet, rebels
are very predictable; they will do the opposite of what you or anyone
else tells them to do! They are "reverse puppets." Reverse puppets are
adults or children who are so visibly discouraged that they are obnoxious, uncooperative, and self-centered. They have no social interest
or at least exhibit very little. Adler believed that all people were born
with an "innate potential" for the social interest. It is still difficult to
determine whether he said this tongue-in-cheek or in philosophical
ambiguity.

It is heartening to witness the extraordinary social interest children
generate when they are given a modest adult model and even minimal
encouragement. When these two ingredients are absent, tremendous
battles for power ensue and, unfortunately, useless behavior is pursued
by both the discouraged adults and children. The following case illustrates such a struggle:

Jack was the five-year-old adopted son of two well-educated adults.
By most standards, the family would be judged capable of reason.

Yet, the desire for power was so pervasive among these three people that the reverse puppet syndrome had grown to malignant proportions.

Both parents had been classroom teachers and saw themselves as firm disciplinarians. They secretly hoped to maintain their same style after they got the baby. Yet, when Jack entered the family, their classroom experience proved ineffective. There weren't any guidelines for controlling the behavior of a three-year-old who wasn't very verbal. To compound the problem further, Mom and Dad didn't child-proof their home which led to excessive "don'ts" and "no's." The restrictions and transgressions multiplied. By the time Mom and Dad reached our counseling center, Jack was five and the parents had an armload of episodes which documented his uncontrollable, belligerent, powerful behavior.

For example, one day Mom was talking to a neighbor on the patio while Jack played inside within her view. As Mom talked, Jack strode brazenly to the refrigerator. "Don't open the refrigerator, Jack," she said. The door swung wide. She nervously carried on the conversation as Jack methodically removed something from the shelf. "Jack, what do you have? Put it back!" Apparently deaf, Jack strode to the sliding glass patio door cradling his prize. "Jack, whatever you do, don't bring it out here!" Delicately cradling his possession in one hand, he opened the sliding door with the other. "Jack, what do you have? I told you not to get in the refrigerator." Jack had retrieved an egg and was quite conscious of its fragile status. "Jack, take it back this instant!" He walked slowly to his mother's side, expressionless. Jack gazed intently at his mother, then at the neighbor, and then back to Mom. "For God sakes, don't drop it!..." Then as if in a dream, he began to turn his hand over, too fast to be stopped and too slow to be accidental: the egg broke open on the toe of Mom's patent leather shoes. Mom went berserk. She sputtered, swatted, and dragged Jack, totally impassive, into the house. Episodes like these became routine. Several months passed before these parents reached the family counseling center. A final episode pushed them to desperation.

One evening Mom insisted that Jack eat a serving of cooked carrots. Jack violently refused. He yelled, banged the table, and cried loudly. Mom stuck to her guns. Jack cried more violently and the carrots were long cold. When Dad questioned the mother's tactics, a fight ensued and Dad stomped out of the house. Jack continued to cry. After two hours Mom went next door to visit friends. An hour passed and she returned. As she approached the front door, she heard nothing. She opened the door cautiously to discover Jack still sitting at the table but silent. As his eyes met hers, he burst into a violent tirade and continued until he fell asleep with his head in the carrots. The next day Jack was voiceless, and Mom wondered about the possibility of permanent damage to his vocal cords. After this ordeal, Mom and Dad began to question their strategies.

Why didn't Jack leave the table after Mom left the house? Was he frightened? That didn't seem likely, given his total disregard for authority. Why was he quiet when she was gone and purposely obnoxious again when she returned? What was he trying to prove? One thing finally appeared clear. She wasn't likely to muscle this youngster into submission. Jack seemed totally unpredictable. Then it occurred to her—he was absolutely predictable. He would always do exactly the opposite of what she commanded. She had discovered the reverse puppet syndrome.

In their belligerence, children lose themselves in their own rebellion. They don't realize that what they seek to avoid most in life, being controlled, is precisely what they bring upon themselves. When parents demand "A" of children, "Z" is certain to follow. When the right arm is pulled, the left raises. When parents demand sitting, the reverse puppet is sure to stand. Each command by an adult generates an opposite reaction by the child. These demands, which are always demands upon others for compliance, set the stage for the inevitable struggle for power and freedom. It is a classic struggle between lords and serfs, but it is difficult to identify who plays which role.

The struggle for power is as futile as the feudal system. Relationships based upon subordination, autocratic rule, and superiority to inferiority are doomed. To combat the reverse puppet syndrome in a family, it is necessary to free both puppet and puppeteer from the strings of illusion; that is, it's vital to understand the operating principles that govern the child's behavior and encourage him or her to choose useful behaviors.

CUTTING THE STRINGS OF ILLUSION

Most of us live under the mistaken belief that we control the behavior of our children. Some of us enjoy this fantasy for briefer periods than others, but all of us court the idea momentarily. Slowly, and in some instances suddenly, we come to grips with reality that Kahlil Gibran offered long ago.

> Your children are not your children. They come through you but not from you; and though they are with you, yet they belong not to you. You may give them love but not your thoughts, for they have their own thoughts. You may house their bodies but not their souls, for their souls dwell in the house of the tomorrow, which you cannot visit, even in your dreams. You may strive to be like them but seek not to make them like you, for life goes not backward nor tarries with yesterday (Gibran, *The Prophet*).

Let's go back to Jack and his family. Both Jack's and his mother's difficulties can be attributed to the false belief each held about the other. Mom assumed that as the parent it was her right and duty to control Jack. Jack figured that might was right as long as might was mighty enough. Each gave the other the illusion of control. Closer inspection revealed the truth. When Mom pulled the string for "sit," Jack stood. When Jack rebelled, he assumed his defiance demonstrated his control. In fact, he was totally controlled. He could be counted on to do the opposite of what he was told to do—like a puppet with faulty rigging.

Breaking their deadlock required major concessions and insights by Mom and Dad and, in the end, courage from Jack. In extreme struggles for power, one side must refuse to fight. At the counseling center Jack's Mom and Dad were given the following advice: the battle for control cannot be waged if one person leaves the field. Mom was not convinced, but she felt defeated, overrun, and threatened. Not surprisingly, Dad, who for years had been leaving the house during conflict, accepted the recommendation readily. Both parents would have to change their lifestyle and tactics.

In this case Mom could not throw in the towel and that is what she needed to do. She had left the house once, and in her mind, it hadn't worked. After all, Jack sat at the table for hours and resumed crying when she walked in the door.

"What does it tell you?" I asked. "Strength, endurance, power, and lack of insight," she replied. She was right about everything but "lack of insight."

"How did you feel when you returned to the house to see Jack sitting at the table?" I asked.

"Defeated," she said. Then, as if hit by a sledgehammer, it occurred to her. Just as she walked into the house, Jack had turned his eyes to hers and smiled slightly, as if to say "I'll show you," then burst into a hoarse cry.

"Could it be," I suggested, "that he had more invested in defeating you than finishing the carrots, or getting down from the table?"

To break the rebellious dance of the marionettes, adults must concede the child's strength without conceding their own rights and dignity. In this particular case, Mom and Dad were told to do the following: 1) remove themselves from situations which did not absolutely require discipline; 2) remove objects, themselves, or Jack instead of commanding obedience; 3) offer Jack choices they (Mom and Dad) were willing to live with; 4) systematically set aside special time for Jack with each parent; and 5) give Jack power in useful situations.

In addition to guidelines, pragmatic alternatives were suggested like walking into the house and locking it if Jack was harassing any adult outside, allowing Jack to go hungry, removing Jack to his room and placing a child-proof knob on the inside to prevent him from leaving until he was ready to cooperate, and declaring a parental bladder attack, retreating to the bathroom when Jack was being demanding and tyrannical.

Jack's parents had the benefit of counseling, but they didn't have what you have now, outlined alternatives and an illustrative case history to assist in the application of the ideas. If you consistently use the strategies outlined above, you probably won't need the help of a counselor. Everything offered here could be generated by you if you apply the concepts of logical consequences. Each family is unique, but also very much like other families. The principles apply to all of us, but we must find their application in unique ways in our own families.

The following week we saw the family again and talked with Jack and Mom and Dad. The following excerpts from the transcripts give insight into Jack's thinking:

> Counselor: Jack, if you could be any kind of animal, what would you choose to be? (Long pause.)
> Jack: Lion.
> Co: Could you tell me about that?
> Jack: It's the king, the toughest and they don't have to work.
> Co: Who's the lion in your house?

Jack: Me.

Co: How are you king?

Jack: Nobody can boss me.

Co: Does that make you feel brave?

Jack: Sometimes.

Co: At times not!

Jack: (Silence.)

Co: I have an idea why that is. Would you like to hear it? (Jack nods affirmatively.) You know what a puppet is and how it works, right? (Jack nods.) Well, the puppeteer tells the puppet to do everything. You are like a reverse or backward puppet. Every time Mom tells you to do something, you are so busy trying to be the boss that you always do the opposite. (Jack smiles.) But it doesn't make you feel brave all the time because sometimes you can't do things you really would like to do because Mom wants you to. You're so busy being a backward puppet and saying "no" to prove you're the boss that you miss out on doing what you want to do.

Jack: Yeah, it's fun but it's not fair.

Co: You feel you lose.

Jack: Yeah.

Co: How would you like things to be different at home?

Jack: Mom yells at me.

Co: And that's unfair and seems to hurt.

Jack: Yes.

Co: Could you help me get Mom to change?

Jack: I don't know.

Co: You're very strong. I'll bet you could.

Jack: (Silence.)

Co: Well, I think that you are too strong for your Mom and Dad and sometimes they are afraid of you. (Jack listens intently.) They try very hard to boss you but they can't. From now on, we are going to tell them to stop trying to boss you because you're too tough for them, but it is not fair for you to boss them either.

When you try, we will tell them to go away, to another room, or outside until you stop bossing. What you will have to do is be your own boss. You will have to decide for yourself what you want to do instead of doing the backward (opposite) of what they tell you. The important thing is that they are not going to fight with you any more. What do you think? (Long, long pause.)

114

Jack: You mean I can do what I want and Mom won't yell?

Co: No, you will have to decide what to do. If it isn't right or if you try to boss Mom, Mom will not yell; but she will leave or ask you to leave.

Jack: What if I won't go?

Co: You may go by yourself or they will take you. If they take you, they will decide when you come back. If you leave by yourself, you can come back when you decide! What's bothering you about this? (Silence.) I have an idea. Would you like to hear it? (Jack nods.) Are you worried about not being with Mom like you have? (Jack seems to be ready to cry.) If not having Mom to yourself bothers you, maybe we need some special time for the two of you. A time for just you and Mom when you can be the boss as long as you're nice to her.

Jack agreed to special time and the new discipline. The parents were told in Jack's presence that things might get worse before they got better until Jack was convinced they were really going to behave differently.

In addition, I asked Dad how Jack used him to become as powerful as Mom. Initially he was confused by my question because he had forgotten about his role in the interaction.

Dad: What do you mean, how do I help him? I don't help him!

Co: Why do I get the feeling you think some of his antics are kind of funny?

Dad: Well, he's so damn quick, just a little pistol.

Co: All boy, huh?

Dad: Yeah, I guess so. (Smiling)

Co: I think so too. And, Jack knows you condone and even support his behavior at times!

Dad: I don't either! I think it's funny, but I don't support it.

Co: Funny—because he does things to Mom you'd like to do?

Dad: You're right! (Dad laughs with some embarrassment)

Co: You do condone and even support him against Mom and you must make your peace with her so Jack can make his. He will know if the two of you have made your peace if you stop running away and stand your ground against him instead of running away.

Dad: I don't like to see my self that way...but maybe you're right.

Co: We will know what you've decided about that by next week, I am sure.

Not long after visiting the counseling center another episode occurred. Dad was watching a football game one evening while Mom was trying to get Jack to bed. Mom had taken Jack to his room, read to him, gotten him a drink, and settled him in for the night twice. Each time he returned to the family room with several toys in tow. Extremely agitated, Mother yelled, "Jack, stay in your room! You're supposed to be in bed, not watching TV."

As she began to scream, Dad stirred and looked as if he was about to bolt for the door. "I think I'll take a walk, do you mind?" Mother asked.

Somewhat startled, Dad agreed, "Well, yeah…Oh, go ahead!" Jack continued crying loudly. Dad carried Jack to his room and tried to comfort him but he had become belligerent. Shortly after Dad returned to the game, Jack was wailing in his ear. Then Dad remembered the child-proof doorknob. "Jack, you can go back to your room by yourself or I'll take you. If I take you I am closing the door and you'll have to stay there until I open it. If you go by yourself, you can leave the door open."

Appearing oblivious to Dad's choice, Jack continued wailing. Dad picked Jack up firmly and took him to his room and closed the door. Jack lay at the foot of the door and cried wildly through the entire first half of the football game. Then things were quiet. Dad went down the hall to check. Jack had fallen asleep on the floor by the door.

The next night Mom was about to go through the same bedtime routine, when Dad suggested that she might like to take a walk instead. Jack looked at Dad with disbelieving eyes. Dad said, "Jack, I'll take you to bed or you can go on your own. If you go on your own, I'll be down in a minute to read to you. If I have to take you, I'll have to close the door." Jack turned and walked immediately to his room. "I'll get the books, Dad." The couple was stunned, but encouraged. Both realized that Jack's behavior was often supported or initiated by one of them. They agreed to work harder to cooperate with one another and felt, somehow, their cooperation would help them win Jack's.

This case illustrates all of the principles suggested in this book. Rebels can't maintain their opposition to you without your participation and cooperation. The effectiveness of these strategies doesn't reside in the cleverness or content of the interventions like the child-proof doorknob, etc., but in recognizing the emotional movement or dynamics between you and your kids. Focusing on the intent of the behavior helps us to see that useless goals aren't about breaking eggs from the refrigerator but about struggles for power, supremacy and belonging. As the case of Jack illustrates, to dissolve the useless goals of children, adults must forfeit their illusions about winning out over the child. You probably don't need professional help to recognize the benefit of abandoning your desire to defeat your child.

Mom and Dad were amazed at the emotional turnaround. It wasn't an instant success story, but the episodes steadily subsided and in a few short months, disappeared entirely. And, occasionally Jack could be heard saying, "Never mind, Mom, I can handle it."

Guidelines for Redirecting Reverse Puppets

1. Remove the child or yourself in heated conflicts for power or supremacy.

2. Offer choices to the children that you are capable of and willing to live with.

3. Do the unexpected. Avoid playing the same old "I win, you lose" game.

4. Systematically encourage children and offer them opportunities for power on the useful side of life.

A FINAL COMMENT

To defuse any power struggle someone has to take the first step, and in the case of your children, it will have to be you. Parents will have power with—but not over—their children when they realize, as Gibran expressed it—

> "You may give them your love but not your thoughts, for they have their own thoughts. You may house their bodies but not their souls, for their souls dwell in the house of tomorrow, which you can never visit..."

10
MORNING GORIES:
Narcolepsy and Other
Morning Sicknesses

It is a surprising but accurate paradox: control is gained by giving it up.

—*F.M.*

There are epidemics of morning sickness around the country, but in most families the nausea is not caused by parents expecting babies—but by parents expecting kids to get out of bed, expecting them to get dressed, to eat breakfast, and get to school on time. Why should such benign transactions become sickening? Because until parents become wiser or the kids older, responsibility for the morning routine usually falls on Mom or Dad.

Parents are often alarm clocks, valets, restauranteurs, appointment secretaries, and chauffeurs. Every family is different, but one thing seems consistent: parents typically assume too much responsibility for their youngsters, and in so doing generate more work for themselves.

NARCOLEPSY—SLEEPING SICKNESS

How do you get your kids up in the morning? If Hollywood would spend as much time dealing with this simple exchange as you have, they would have the material for a great situation comedy.

The Coma Brothers

John and Nancy were the parents of two boys, ages seven and ten, who were very heavy sleepers. John assumed responsibility for getting the boys up in the morning because they were so difficult to rouse. He felt it was a genetic condition—Nancy was the same way. Most mornings, he was annoyed by 7:00, angry by 7:15, and furious by 7:30. Both boys seemed to lapse into a coma at dawn, and he felt like he was trying to raise the dead. The older boy was easier to rouse than the younger, but both required loud talk, repeated trips to the bedroom, pulling the covers off, and even dumping mattresses on the floor. It wasn't until Dad was obviously angry that the boys moved in earnest. The routine had become a chronic crisis that soured the day before it started.

Judging by the anger Dad felt, it is safe to assume that the boys were overpowering him. Since Dad had assumed responsibility for the boys' consciousness, he was doomed to defeat. I spoke to the boys and my suspicions were confirmed. The boys weren't interested in sleeping longer, just in showing Dad that he couldn't wake them. When Dad heard the boys admit that it was kind of fun, he was angry all over again. However, his anger solidified his will to change. The boys were reasonably sure they could wake themselves if properly prepared, although the younger was hesitant.

Following the principles for generating encouragement, Mom and Dad established the following interventions:

1. First they informed the boys at a neutral time that they, Dad and Mom, wouldn't nag them any more about getting out of bed in the morning. John and Nancy assumed that the boys were old enough to wake themselves and told them so.

2. Secondly, the parents backed up their words of encouragement with concrete action. Since the boys were old enough to get themselves up, they were old enough to have their own alarm clock. John and Nancy turned the alarm clock purchase into a mini special tme. They also made an effort to spend special time with each child individually; in addition, they scheduled time as a family.

   The boys were both given power on the useful side of life. A key was placed in a secret hiding place known only to them; if they ever needed to get into the house, they had their own secret key.

3. Finally, the boys were given the choice of going to church or Sunday school on Sundays. In the past John and Nancy had tried to force

the boys to go to Sunday school and usually Sunday morning ended in a war. (Someone once said that parents are never closer to hell than they are on Sunday morning when they are trying to get their kids to church!) On the first Sunday exercising their new choice, the boys decided to go to church. The sermon wasn't particularly geared to them, but strangely enough they listened, seemed to enjoy being with Mom and Dad and, surprisingly, made comments or asked questions about the sermon as the day passed. John and Nancy were a little bewildered, but pleasantly surprised.

These encouragement strategies, as much as any logical consequences, seemed to improve the boys' behavior. And when you think about it, in our society responsibility is fostered by increased choice, independence, and responsibility—not regulations and constraints.

The guidelines for sleeping sickness must be tailored specifically to fit the useless misbehavior and the family situation. In this case, since both boys were driven to school by Dad, the following recommendations were provided:

1. John and Nancy were to inform the boys at a neutral time that they would no longer nag the boys about getting out of bed.

2. They were to make bags for the boys with their names on them. If they had to leave the house before they dressed, their clothes were to be placed in the bag and taken to the car. Then, the boys had the choice of dressing in the car or when they arrived at their destination. (Older children could be left at home, but the children and the school should know that you, their parents, are not excusing them.)

3. Nancy and John were to encourage both youngsters, assuring them that they could get themselves up now that they had their own alarm clock.

4. They were to inform the boys that no breakfast would be served past 8:10 A.M.. Therefore, if they planned to eat, they must be up and dressed by that time.

5. The parents were to make it clear to the boys that, by law, they were required to take them to school, but whether the boys learned or graduated was up to them.

While these logical consequences were being employed, an effort was made to encourage each child. The "coma brothers" rapidly developed consciousness. Although Dad had to carry the older brother's shoes and shirt to the car once, the boy was dressed before the car left the neighborhood. For the most part, both boys enjoyed the responsibility of getting themselves up and avoiding the morning hassle with Dad. As an added benefit, they seemed to get to the table earlier and eat better. And, as things became more relaxed, Dad and the boys actually began to talk to one another. In less than two weeks, this family turned around a useless long-term tradition.

Guidelines for Sleeping Sickness

1. Make a hard assessment of those things you do in the name of being a "good" parent.

2. Turn the responsibility for getting up over to the children and hold them accountable.

3. Buy an alarm clock and make it an encouraging experience for the children.

4. Serve notice of your retirement as morning maid, valet, and appointment secretary.

5. Anticipate logical consequences and generate disciplinary alternatives in advance.

6. Provide special time and encouragement on a negotiated basis to fill the gap of lost attention, affection, and services.

SCHOOL PHOBIA

If a child is actually frightened or sick at the thought of going to school, the behavior may serve a different purpose. Phobic reactions are as purposeful as sleeping sickness, but more intense. Extreme fear, or phobia, relieves the child of responsibilities and usually indentures one or more family members. In this way powerlessness begets power. But this overstatement of emotion is symptomatic of unhealthy alliances in the family. Therefore, if this happens in your family, interventions should focus on your family interactions, not just the child. The next case history may serve to illustrate.

Jessie, age thirteen, had begun to be sick every morning before school. The family had moved to the community about six months prior to the onset of these episodes and Jessie's mother Joan had been struggling in recent months to make a career decision. Upon arriving at school, Jessie became quite sick: nauseous, dizzy, and pale. Her parents were called and her mother would come and take her home. Mom would care for Jessie until she was better, which usually occurred about mid-afternoon. At home Jessie moved around the house freely, watching T.V., reading magazines, and sleeping. Mother nursed her with concern and tried to soothe her vague anxieties.

During a joint family session when Joan's career was discussed, the purposefulness of their joint behavior became apparent. Jessie said, "When I sit there in school studying algebra, I feel very sad and miss you terribly, Mom." Jessie identified her sadness as empathy for her mother's struggle with her career decision as well as a sense of loneliness which she projected to Mom. Jessie was very self-assured in her own career choice; she wanted to be a chemist, but she felt guilty about her mother's indecisiveness and apparent isolation in their new community.

"Why can't Mom just be happy being Mom? I need her to be just Mom for awhile." I suggested that Jessie's phobia was an attempt to rescue her mother, below her awareness, by being sick and in need of care, by being home in need of nurturing—by being Mom's little girl again. Instead of defining Jessie as immature, manipulative or frightened, I suggested that she was actually demonstrating her compassion for Mom's lonely and difficult predicament. Instead of defining Jessie's behavior as bad, juvenile, or sick, it was re-labeled "well intended" but useless. Thus, Jessie didn't have to feel defensive about her fears or immaturity, nor did she have to feel guilty; by reframing her behavior, her natural inclination to resist change was diffused.

At this point, Joan was asked to give Jessie permission to be a chemist and to go to school. If Jessie came home sick, Joan was to allow Jessie to care for herself as much as possible. Jessie was told, paradoxically, not to force herself to go to school. "Stay home as long as you like. In fact, if you feel like going back, check with us (at the counseling center) first. We don't want you to return prematurely." While at home, Jessie was to behave as if she were sick or in school. If she was sick, she was to be in her room resting without radio or T.V. If she felt better, she was to act as if she were in school and study, but not go to school. Mom was instructed, paradoxically, to focus on helping Jessie instead of forcing herself to choose a career.

After several days at home Jessie was bored and eager to go back to school. Joan wasn't providing much service, but she had sabotaged the counseling recommendations about focusing on Jessie's independence by going to a career counselor.

Jessie was asked to stay home until the following week and to come home at noon on her first day back. By Tuesday of the second week, Jessie was back to full attendance and Joan had applied to law school. Most importantly, both had changed the way they behaved toward one another. Jessie was more overtly annoyed with her mother and less depressed. Joan, by comparison, was less reactive to Jessie's sadness but seemed to like her better—and seemed to like herself better as well.

Symptoms like these are usually mutually generated. Jessie and Joan gave each other what they needed. Jessie needed phobia to keep her mother as "Mom," and Joan needed Jessie's dependence to give herself permission to stay home—to stay "Mom."

Parents can't be expected to dig out the diagnostic complexities of Jessie's case and find the exact parallel in their own situations. However, the case gives all of us a set of principles which should generalize to many similar circumstances. What does Jessie's case tell us?

1. Sudden onset of school phobia or problems in the morning are probably triggered by events at home as well as school. All behavior takes place in a social context. Phobic behavior, more than other run-of-the-mill useless goals, involves problem behavior of the identified child and one or two other specific people. In other words, the phobic reaction is a particular response to a specific relationship.

2. Involved parents must avoid being professional enablers, that is, doing things for the "sick" kid which further incapacitate or coddle the child.

3. Most importantly, parents of phobic kids must stop acting as if the agent responsible for the child's condition is outside the family. They must acknowledge that the problem is almost always generated by friction between the child and themselves.

4. If there is any doubt about the effectiveness of the efforts to help correct the situation, parents should get professional help. It's not advisable to plod along hoping things will change.

The guidelines offered here are just that, guidelines. If you aren't able to nip excessive fears about school in the bud, don't procrastinate—get professional help immediately. All behavior is purposeful. Your interventions must, therefore, include change for you and your child.

Guidelines for School Phobia

1. Get professional help for school or other phobic problems.

2. Don't move too quickly to change the child. Instead, watch yourself for awhile.

RIDING HERD OVER THE LITTLE DAWDLERS

Parents are often exhausted by the demands of infant care, but the truth is that once kids are up and about, parenting has just begun. Corraling and herding little dawdlers has proved to be a recurring problem for many families. The causes for dawdling are many and as usual can be attributed to the useless goals of children and the psychological priorities of adults.

For most of America's children the morning routine doesn't require the physical labor and time it used to—no cows to milk or horses to feed. Kids have few responsibilities beyond their own personal hygiene. As a result, they're unoccupied and underfoot.

About a decade ago parents began to rely upon the electronic pacifier—the television—as a means of coping with preschool kids in the morning. Captain Kangaroo was Mom and Dad's nomination for Emmy in the category of best use of video for visual pacification. Parents credited the Captain and Mr. Green Jeans for the luxury of dressing without an audience.

We are the first generation of parents to use, and probably abuse, kiddy video. Since we are cutting new ground here, it's impossible to anticipate the problems that television fixation or saturation might impose. However, other problems are abundantly clear! Once our preschoolers are school-aged and bound by schedules that have to be coordinated with our own, we're in trouble. Let's say the kids have to catch the bus at 7:35 A.M. and we have to be in our own car pool by 7:40. Here it is 7:25 and we're scrambling around frantically trying to get our kids dressed, fed, and out the door—but they're lying in their P.J.'s in front of the T.V., watching Mr. Rogers sing about his neighborhood! As 7:35 approaches, panic replaces frenzy, and we yell as only adults can, "Don't you care what time it is?" Clever! After six years of kiddy video, they don't know or care. They're doing exactly what we've trained them to do.

Morning lethargy is a product of adult's and children's useless behavior. Parents have become accustomed to believing they are entitled to comfort and privacy in their own home. The goal is appropriate and deserved, but the means of attaining it has been misguided. Children, on the other hand, expect independence and dignity. Imagine that! However, like adults, kids employ useless methods of acquiring the independence and dignity they deserve. Just as adults attempt to control, kids try to get attention by subordinating parents and siblings while assuming little responsibility.

The first step in derailing the useless behaviors of the dawdler or slowpoke is to recognize that they have been created and supported by parents and children. Maybe you didn't use the T.V. "pacifier," but you may still have a covey of dawdlers. The dawdler raises strong feelings of frustration and annoyance in adults. These emotions help us to identify the useless goal as an attention-getting mechanism.

Most dawdling is a product of parental indulgence, excessive childhood expectations, and inadequate training. Since dawdling takes place around morning chores and responsibilities, logical consequences must be generated for each episode, but general guidelines can be developed. There are a few realities which can serve as springboards for logical consequences. For example, contemporary parents are often working parents and must leave the house to work, so kids must go to school or be home alone and truant.

The consequences of dawdling, such as tardiness, absence, etc., usually fall upon the adult. But if children are given choices within limits, the responsibility can be shifted from adults to children. For example, parents don't have to force children to eat breakfast. Kids can go temporarily hungry if they like. However, if they choose to eat, they must (if it is a reasonable family rule) be completely dressed to eat. Children don't have to wear color-coordinated Geranimals or what mother demands they wear. However, they must be dressed.

Kids who can't get two pieces of clothing on in the proper order, like socks and shoes, try our souls. But remember, helplessness results

126

in someone taking responsibility for dressing the child. Personal service is the goal of the dawdler! So, it's important not to give in at these critical times! At a neutral time, we must train the child, but not at 8:30 A.M. Monday morning. At that time of day, it's time for action, not words.

For wardrobe selection, the youngster can make a choice within reasonable, established limits. "You may wear anything that you like from the clean clothes drawer—you decide." It's not necessary to make a war out of wardrobe selection. If you consider for a moment how silly it is for you to be fighting with someone about what s/he should wear, it's easy to stop. Consider saying the same thing to your mate as he or she dresses in the morning. What kind of reaction would you get?

Once you have taken the battle out of selecting the wardrobe, the last step for derailing dawdlers is to remove yourself from the war against the clock and the child. "You don't seem to be ready. I guess you have decided to finish dressing in the car/bus on the way to school. The choice is yours. Dress here or there." Quietly put the rest of the youngster's clothes in a paper bag with his/her name on it and carry the bag to the car if necessary. I have never known a youngster who wound up at school undressed. Consistency usually shortens the process by convincing the youngsters that you are really going to let them handle it. After a few days, kids will be washing, eating, and dressing promptly.

The key is providing choices, choices youngsters and parents can accept without sacrificing dignity. A summary of the tactical strategies for sleeping sickness, school phobia, dawdling, dressing, and eating might be as follows:

1. Children must go to school or be home alone and truant.
2. Children don't have to eat. Parents are obligated to provide food, but not obligated to force feed children.
3. Children's attire doesn't have to be perfect. You can be comfortable with a child's own choices if you remember that clothes are not a reflection on your ability to parent.
4. Follow through with the options you provide. Even if it threatens to be embarrassing, it won't be catastrophic.
5. Don't give in. By standing your ground, you demonstrate self-respect.

6. Don't serve the child. By allowing the child to overcome this mild adversity, you show respect for his/her ability.

7. Act, don't talk.

8. Make time for training.

JUVENILE HARDENING OF THE ARTERIES: FORGETFULNESS

"Polly, did you remember your coat? How about your spelling words? Don't forget your books. Do have your lunch? I don't suppose you remembered your milk money! Isn't today Brownies? ...Honestly, you would forget your head if it weren't attached."

This original quote reflects a textbook example of juvenile hardening of the arteries with early onset—Polly is age seven. This isn't a new phenomenon, but whenever it happens to us it feels like there is an epidemic. Having tried to shift the responsibility for the condition to anyone or anything else but ourselves, we have only to replay a portion of the opening dialogue to discover the origin. "Don't forget your books. Do you have your lunch?..." Polly remembers nothing because Polly has had to remember nothing! Her short-term memory has atrophied through lack of use. Why remember anything? Everything is remembered for her. Constantly reminding kids and taking responsibility for them is extremely debilitating and discouraging.

If you have difficulty empathizing with that statement, try to remember again how you feel when your spouse nags you about something you fully intended to do, or wanted to forget. In either case, it is annoying and unnecessary. The effect on children is devastating. The child becomes an adult who believes s/he is incapacitated, and usually finds a mate that is eager to support these inadequacies as a means of insuring his or her own need to be needed. Supporting juvenile hardening of the arteries serves no good purpose, especially considering how easy it is to change the situation.

Pumping New Blood

Let's look at Polly again. She can help us trace the roots of effective discipline and encouragement. What would the consequences have been if Polly forgot some or all of those things her mother remembered for her? In the past, it meant more work for Mom. When Polly forgot her milk money, lunch sack, and Brownie outfit, Mom brought them to school for her. Without realizing it, Mother had taken on the duties of a delivery service.

Polly rarely left the house without what she needed because her mother was always at the door to insure survival between school and home. On occasion, gloves, tennis shoes, etc., were left behind, so mother, being a "good Mom," delivered them to school.

At times Polly remembered, usually when no one was there to do it for her, and at times she didn't. But when Polly forgot, the consequences didn't affect her, just her mother.

Treating kids like amnesia victims is destructive. Yet, this is one of the easiest problems to deal with if parents would simply retire from the servitude they have grown accustomed to. Retiring from service dramatically shifts responsibility. Consider the alternatives. If Polly forgets her milk money or Brownie outfit, and Mother refuses to bring them to school special delivery, what happens? Clearly, the consequences would be far from catastrophic, inconvenient at most.

Also, what impact would the inconvenience have on Polly's short-term memory? In my experience, these discomforts have a powerful way of jogging the synapses, dramatically improving short-term memory. Also, by shifting responsibility to the child, motivation is altered, thus paving the way for behavior change. Behavior will change only when motivation has changed.

Polly's inattention can be dealt with by allowing the natural consequences to jog her memory. The former is a preferred consequence, but when parents worry about doctor bills and medical expenses, setting limits can work. If Polly leaves without a coat, she should not be allowed to play outside during recess or go to any extracurricular activities. Other limits could be imposed to reduce parental concern. But, whenever possible, let the elements instruct the child about appropriate apparel. In most other instances, if parents stop serving the youngster, memory will improve dramatically.

Guidelines for Forgetfulness

1. Announce your intentions to retire from nagging and serving the child.

2. Shift responsibility for forgetfulness by recognizing who owns the problem and who pays the price for forgetfulness.

3. For adolescents, set limits and restrict mobility by withdrawing financial support of irresponsible behavior.

4. Notify the child that you intend to retire as servant and valet, but you would be happy to do things with and for them at a negotiated time.

TEENAGE SENILITY

Forgetfulness isn't the exclusive prerogative of young children. Adolescents can have chronic arterial sclerosis if the problems aren't addressed at an early age. Perhaps one area where adolescent hardening of the arteries is most apparent is the use of the family automobile(s). "I forgot to put gas in it. I didn't know it was empty." "I didn't see the stop sign."

Automobiles strike the fear of God in parents, but never kids. Kids don't seem to be frightened by anything. Most parents try to handle these fears by placing constraints on driving and, as a result, cars become just another power issue. By comparison, if parents treat automobiles like opportunities and responsibilities to be shared, punitive constraints can be minimized.

Teenage Drivers

Cars cost money. This simple truth is the foundation for logical consequences and responsible behavior. If parents act "as if" driving is a privilege and responsibility, the situation doesn't have to become an ordeal. Set the stage early. As youngsters approach driving age, share their excitement, encourage learner's permits and driver's education.

Since your insurance will go up when the young person begins driving, s/he ought to share in that expense. However, in most states insurance companies offer reduced rates for students who have completed driver's education, so you can pass this financial break on to the child. The amount of insurance the child has to pay ought to be balanced with the amount of time s/he has to devote to work at the expense of extra curricular activities. A car ought not interfere with a youngster's opportunity to debate, act, or play cello or football. The exact amount of the child's contribution can be negotiated at a family meeting.

Some system ought to be negotiated to cover driving expenses. If the youngster does errands for the family, these can be balanced against those times s/he utilizes the car for pleasure. Some families have established a weekly fee for automobile use. This eliminates arguments about empty gas tanks and distance traveled. Other families use a pay-as-you-go plan, using odometer readings to charge kids for the use of the car. Although this is workable there is some game playing that can be done with this technique. The basic philosophy which ought to guide decisions is that cars cost money to buy, run, and maintain and kids must share in the expense as well as the pleasure. By the same token, if parents expect kids to assume responsibility for driving, adults can't arbitrarily use youthful drivers for their own convenience, running errands, driving carpools, etc. The critical work here is "arbitrary." Parents should strive for democratic and prearranged agreements.

Cars are fun, provide freedom of movement and adventure. They are also tedious, inconvenient, dirty, and boring. When possible, kids should learn how to and help change the oil, rotate tires, and all the other things that take up either Saturday afternoons or money or both. If you have a choice of paying to have routine maintenance done or doing it yourself with your children, choose the latter. It's another opportunity your kids have to learn responsibility.

These suggestions presume that the vehicle being driven is yours. If possible, keep it that way. When high school kids can afford their own cars, it means they're working too much and aren't involved in school. If youngsters own their own car, do everything you can to insure that they have all the freedom and "all" the responsibility.

Guidelines for Using the Family Car

1. Have the youngster share financial responsibility for driving the family car. This could include: 1) insurance; 2) maintenance; 3) operating costs; 4) violations and accidents.

2. Balance privilege with responsibility. Running errands for parents can be weighed against driving the car for personal use.

131

3. Set limits in advance to avoid arbitrary constraints.

4. Discourage teenagers from owning their own vehicles.

To summarize, adolescents are less likely to be forgetful and irresponsible about gasoline, changing oil, and reckless driving if they have responsibility for these things. As youngsters approach adulthood, the message of this book becomes intensified, "You can't assume responsibility for things that aren't your responsibility." You can't prevent your sixteen-year-old son from speeding nor can you prevent him from having his license revoked. You can deny him the use of your car, increase his insurance, or refuse to sign bank notes, charge mileage, etc. But in the final analysis, you can't drive for your teenage son or daughter. Only the adolescent can drive carefully and responsibly.

THE TENDER TRAP

Most of us have fallen into the trap of using our children to fulfill our own emotional needs. We deny our selfish motives through the transparent nobility of being a "good" parent. It's hard to accept ourselves as selfish until we see how, under the guise of "perfect parenting," we strip our kids of independence and autonomy. Never do for children what they can do for themselves. "Never" isn't an injunction as much as it is an encouraging reminder. Sometimes we can't help ourselves, sometimes we do for them by choice. For those occasions the rule of thumb is to serve them and enjoy it, but don't make a habit of it.

11
THE SUPPER SUICIDE HOUR:
Yuk, Not That Again!

Pursuing self-esteem through the stomachs of our
children is nonsense.

—F.M.

Between the hours of 3:45 and 7:00 P.M., incredible things happen in kitchens across the country. It's the time when parent, partner, and child descend upon one another after the day's turmoil. Everyone has an agenda or need that yearns to be met. Adults are in as much need as children.

Let's set the stage. If Mom is already home or is the first to arrive, she usually begins preparing the meal. The children arrive simultaneously, needing emotional and nutritional sustenance. Dad is due shortly and everyone has after-dinner activities scheduled at different times. The person usually responsible for coordinating this nightmare is Mom. Logistically, the task is similar to the Normandy invasion and emotionally it ranks with Guadalcanal.

OH YUK, NOT THAT AGAIN!

With Herculean energy Mom (or Dad) finishes cooking. But as soon as the meal has been placed on the table, someone groans ungratefully, "Oh yuk, not that again!" This response is not restricted to children; at times it can be uttered by one's spouse. There doesn't seem to be any correlation between "Oh yuk" and the amount of time devoted to meal preparation either. In fact, these comments are often leveled when we have slaved to prepare something "special." When the youngest child says, "Oh yuk," it may sound cute, but when your mate utters the phrase, it's time to retire. Regardless of your gender, the notion of the perfect parent as someone capable of and responsible for the culinary satisfaction of everyone is discouraging!

The idea, as expressed on T.V., goes like this—parents who slave their way into culinary oblivion will be guaranteed eternal domestic bliss. All this just by baking the right bundt cake! Furthermore, such people will be doused magically with some exotic mist that will ooze from them along with the smell of fresh baked goods. Thus, when a bundt cake promises domestic bliss, "Oh, yuk" isn't simply a rejection of the menu, but a rejection of one's very sensual and parental being. Somehow, it seems we parents have bought this idea and live in fear of burning the bundt cake. If we fail this one all-consuming mission, we're liable to be rejected by our mate and children who apparently are gourmets by heredity.

Logical Consequences

Pursuing self-esteem through the intestines of others is useless. Laying one's self-esteem at the mercy of a child's digestive system is suicidal. If you recognize the futility of this injunction, it's easy to unchain yourself.

Using encouragement and logical consequences, you can defuse this nightly powder keg by taking the following steps: 1) Announce at a neutral time that you won't assume responsibility for planning the entire weekly menu. Indeed, you could suggest that it may even have been unfair of you to be so presumptuous. Ask that a time be set aside for the family to plan the menu for the week. 2) Each member will be given a choice of meals once a week. In this way, no favorites are played and a sense of fairness is created. 3) On those evenings when the meal served doesn't meet the approval of a particular member, the cook will assume that person won't eat unless otherwise informed. 4) Members choosing not to eat the prepared meal are welcome to abstain, as long as they assume responsibility for feeding themselves without incurring any additional expense. No one should be allowed to prepare a separate, expensive meat dish in lieu of that being served. This usually establishes PBJ's as the alternative. 5) If someone has agreed to the menu and still complains on the evening it's served after he has asked to be included, the options are obvious: (a) ask the complainer to leave the table or (b) remove his plate. Throughout this process, choices can be offered. For example, "I thought you had asked to be included. If you are dissatisfied, I can take your plate. You decide." In this way the person who doesn't want to eat always has alternatives and doesn't have to be cornered.

There are a myriad of variations on this theme. As long as the principles of logical consequences and encouragement are employed, reasonable solutions can be generated. In order to take action in these situations it's important to remember those emotions which trap us initially. Perfect parenting and perfect marriages can't be forged through other people's appetites.

Snacks

Most of our schedules are chaotic. This chaos throws the evening supper hour into such turmoil that it can rarely be referred to as "dinner"—that's far too civilized. These erratic schedules force parents, usually Mom, to set up defensive perimeters around kitchen supplies. Ravenous youngsters swipe at the refrigerator, cupboard, and microwave in highly synchronized movements. Envelopments are launched with perfect timing. Mom can be caught in a crossfire with her hand in the refrigerator and her foot in the cupboard; she can be trapped in verbal skirmishes as well. Whether it is Mom or Dad caught in the defensive encampment, the results are the same. Kids clearly hold parents at bay in kitchens across the country and parents don't realize they have placed themselves in captivity. These antics are usually either attention-getting mechanisms or power struggles. Snacking problems can fall into both of these categories and consequences can be tailored to contend with them.

"Mom, kin I have..." is usually based upon either nutritional or emotional hunger, and parents don't have to be terribly sophisticated to distinguish between the two. By 3:45 P.M., children have developed large dark circles under their eyes and their stomachs can be heard growling in the entry way. If your favorite saying is, "You'll spoil your dinner," it probably falls upon empty stomachs and deaf ears. The absurdity of the statement can only be appreciated when heard in all of its glory. "You'll ruin your dinner." Why is that exactly? After swallowing a piece of cheese at 3:45 P.M., does it sour everything eaten after? Is there a tiny watch smith located in our child's esophagus who knows exactly when and what is ingested and poisons everything before 3:30 and passes everything after 6:00?

It's fair to assume that a modest snack will not devastate his or her finely tuned digestive system. In short, there are legitimate requests which can be honored without falling victim to demands for attention or service. The critical component here is to avoid autocratic confrontations. It's simply not necessary to place yourself between the food and your ravenous children.

Once you recognize that you need not, and cannot, assume responsibility for counting calories or preparing impromptu meals, you can diffuse the "kin I have" statement by implementing logical consequences like the following: 1) In everyone's presence announce that you will no longer battle the youngsters over snacks; 2) indicate to the kids that you will provide the ingredients for a short snack, but you will no longer be nagged into preparing a special pre-meal snack; 3) inform the kids that certain ingredients will be provided so long as they clean up after themselves; 4) tell them that a reasonable quantity will be provided; and once that is consumed, no amount of whining will augment the basic allotment; 5) while the youngsters sit briefly to inhale their interim meal, sit with them and give them your undivided attention for five minutes. Rather than asking them about their day, ask if they would like to hear about yours. By doing this, you will defuse a great deal of bedlam that ensues during the suicide hour. As you immerse yourself in a five-minute mini-special time, you will notice children demanding less of you but sharing more. In this way you can transform a demand for attention into a short encouragement encounter; 6) if you are having difficulty with children eating during the regularly scheduled meal, eating disorders or binge eating, then snacks may not be possible. But, if snack warfare breaks out only during the late afternoon, then it is reasonable to assume that the need is for attention or legitimate hunger.

If you question these recommendations, it's probably because bids for attention have escalated to struggles for power. When this happens, don't hold yourself captive in your own kitchen. A series of choices can be generated.

Children, like plants, need the water of encouragement and the food of life—responsibility, according to Dreikurs. By doing the unexpected, we provide both. Suppose youngsters fail to clean up after themselves. The solution: 1) remove all snackable delicacies from the kitchen before the next day; and 2) once your children begin to nag, remove yourself from the kitchen, serving notice to your children and spouse that you will not prepare meals so long as harassment continues—the choice is theirs. In order to remove yourself, you may have to take a ride in the car or on your bike. You won't have to do this too often to get your message across.

It is important to keep your intentions and actions congruent. You must be fair and firm. To be fair you must serve notice to the youngsters about your intentions. To be firm, you must exert your own need for dignity and respect. Don't shackle yourself to the stove by assuming responsibility as chief cook and bottle washer. If this has happened, a temporary walk-out may be instructive. Don't be guilted into good motherism/dadism. Good parents are parents who refuse to allow their youngsters to be pampered or tyrannical, and that often requires doing the unconventional thing. These recommendations are not acceptable if you are having significant problems with "making" kids eat what's good for them during the scheduled meal. If you are experiencing stomach struggles, to be discussed next, your strategies will have to be modified.

STOMACH STRUGGLES: EATING DIFFICULTIES

Our nation is one of the few which has the luxury of glamorizing a thin body. Only in a society where food is available in abundance can food become a psychological tool of the individual. On the other hand, only in third world countries where food is scarce can it become a political weapon of many. Unfortunately, our society and its commercialism has set paradoxical standards of oral excess and thinness.

On one hand, everyone knows that "nothin' says loving like somethin' from the oven"; on the other hand, no one can deny the eroticism of a one-calorie cola. The social message conveyed by the media is mixed and pervasive. As it is portrayed, love, affection, and erotica can all be experienced through the Pillsbury doughboy; but following our binge, somehow we must be exhorted to thinness by taking pills, joining a spa, or chugging diet soda.

Every time food becomes an issue at the dinner table, parents have either allowed the children to make it an issue, or they've manufactured it themselves. Stomach trouble or stomach struggle, as we'll call it, is always a struggle for power. Once again, children are rapidly aware of those aspects of their lives over which adults have no control. Not surprisingly, they soon recognize those physiological processes which they alone control. Bowel, bladder, and states of consciousness are things over which only the child has control. Eating problems—either the failure to eat or eating to excess—are manifestations of the same issue. Severe difficulties, such as anorexia and bulimia, which eventually become pathological are also related to power and control. Our focus here, however, is designed to handle routine eating problems. The more serious problems will be addressed later.

Fetishes about food usually don't develop without parents providing the idea. Parents begin early with the propaganda. Several years ago it was, "Eat your spinach so you'll grow up to be strong like your Daddy." Today, the message is virtually the same, only the language has changed. "Eat plenty of fiber and don't eat any sugar and you'll grow up to be fit like your Dad."

It is a time-honored tradition that parents should keep watch over their youngsters' nutrition. However, parental obligations might be measured, instead, against their ability to train children to make good dietary decisions on their own, rather than someone else making decisions for them. Eating difficulties aren't to be taken lightly, because they can swell into full-blown pathology. Yet, eating problems usually begin in benign ways. To demonstrate the seriousness of the problem without losing our sense of humor consider the following case history.

Mom and Dad came to the counseling center in great anguish. The initial problem seemed quite innocuous but as data was gathered, things became more involved. Both parents were college-educated, one holding an advanced degree. Dad was a professional communicator and his description of Mom was fluid and entertaining. Mom was robust, funny, and dedicated. The primary complaint was that Susan, their four-year-old daughter, was out of control at mealtime. She refused to eat anything that was prepared for her. During the last month and a half she had lost ten pounds, had been to a physician, and was rapidly approaching serious difficulties.

Mom and Dad had always experienced difficulty with Susan at mealtimes and became accustomed to preparing special menus, but these didn't seem to make any difference. Both parents routinely coaxed and bribed her through meals. She ate less and less. Aside from habitually serving Susan's plate, both parents cut her food and pleaded with her to eat. Finally, they were so desperate they began to punish her, not allowing her to leave the table until she ate, or sending her to her room, etc. She ate even less!

One evening, in exasperation, Mom grabbed Susan by the face and manually operated the mandible and crucible while Dad forced in the food. Brilliant! Having a college degree is obviously no insurance against parental absurdity. Of course, Susan regurgitated everything. Amazingly, this episode isn't what brought this couple to the center. Sadly, it was after Mom had to spank her.

Susan had refused her mother's command and ran defiantly into the yard. Mom, being quite athletic, sprinted after her. The little girl was overtaken near the garden. Mom threw Susan over her knee and grabbed the first switch available. Each time she swatted the child, the switch went unsatisfyingly limp and she would grab another and another and another. As her rage subsided, the mother realized that her switches had been stalks of rhubarb. In her fury, she had destroyed the entire crop. Susan jumped from her knee, smiled belligerently, and strode brazenly away. At this point, and only at this point, did Mom realize that she was powerless in the face of this four-year-old child. This case has always been instructive for parents because of its graphic humor and humility. There is a bit of this mother in all of us.

Eating difficulties that surface as benign attention-getting mechanisms can escalate into full-blown power struggles with blinding speed. Suitable logical consequences and encouragement strategies flow naturally from these conditions if we realize that eating, digestion, and defecation are beyond our power to control. Having recognized and emotionally assessed our powerlessness in these cases, we can turn to consequences and encouragement with enlightened optimism.

Susan's parents, like many of us, took far too much responsibility for their daughter's digestion. Often adults arbitrarily determine not only the menu, but also the quantity of food to be eaten. "Before you get dessert, you must eat four bites of meat and your peas." Sounds reasonable enough, but consider saying the same thing to a guest for Sunday dinner. In this context, the comment is obviously absurd. The difference, of course, rests in the amount of responsibility we assume for another's digestion.

Parents often assume responsibility for serving children their portions "If I didn't put it on their plate, they wouldn't eat it." Parents think that if children weren't served, they would starve or be malnourished. But parents rarely finish this irrational thought..."They are incapable of selecting anything that would keep them alive." However, research has indicated that if children are fed smorgasbord style for extended periods, over time they eat well-balanced diets—very well-balanced diets.

The most fatal parental injunction is, "Try it, it's good for you!" This is guaranteed to kill any child's appetite. The less we lecture about vegetables, the less of an issue they become. We forget that when we prepare our food, we prepare what we like. We neglect to offer children the same rights we enjoy. Tastes, like every aspect of personality, are uniquely developed. Knowing this, we have the rudiments of a logical consequence at our disposal.

1. Allow children to share in the menu-planning process and to serve themselves as long as they eat what they take. (If the child's resistance is deeply entrenched, this alternative may have to be preceded by another alternative to be discussed shortly.) Parents fail to see what supports the struggle over food. Rarely are spinach, carrots, or liver the issue; rather it's the adult's insistence upon eating them that is. Battles ensue over power, not potatoes! Offering children power and dignity to choose is likely to defuse petty bickering and carping.

2. Do not comment about the relative merits of one food over another.

3. Don't fight with children about eating A or B. If a youngster says, "I don't want A," the best response is, "Fine, just don't take any." Don't debate with kids about food "goodness."

4. Never prepare any special or additional food for a child because s/he refuses to eat what is being served.

5. Don't provide between-meal snacks if a child chooses not to eat what is served at mealtime. In this case, the next meal is at the scheduled time and not a minute before.

By now, the consequences are becoming obvious. The most effective teacher is the child's own physiology—hunger. When parents put themselves between the child and these natural consequences, they deprive the child of a most valuable lesson.

These recommendations seem so straightforward that it is difficult to believe they can work, The fact is, they work time and time again. In response to these suggestions, parents occasionally generate another Mack-truck response, "If we don't tell them, they will eat garbage or nothing at all. You mean just let them eat what they want to?" The initial idea is so simple that it is very difficult for parents to accept its credibility. Remarkably, if parents remove their power from the situation, the struggle subsides. Looking back at the case of Susan will illustrate the use of these recommendations nicely.

1. First, Mom and Dad were asked to refrain from serving Susan's plate.

2. The parents were also asked to set aside a time for meal planning.

3. No between-meal treats were to be served. Not surprisingly, the babysitter had no difficulty with Susan during lunch, while Mom and Dad both anguished at breakfast and dinner.

4. In addition, we suggested that if Susan insisted on creating chaos over a particular food she had served herself, she would be excused from the table or her plate could be removed (logical consequences).

Predictably, Susan tried to manufacture struggles within these constraints. Upon initiating these recommendations, Susan refused to eat at all during breakfast and complained bitterly about the food she took during dinner. She ate very little for three days and actually played with and threw food on one occasion. When this occurred, her plate was promptly removed, but she had a standing invitation to return if she chose to cooperate. On the fourth day, she ate until she was full from what was offered but restricted her intake to potatoes and bread. During the second week, the "scenes" had disappeared but she still ate sparingly. As Susan's attempts to overpower her parents became more futile, she ate more. As the parents became more aware of their role in Susan's stomach struggles, her diet became more balanced.

Indeed, as Mom and Dad observed Susan's efforts to draw them into her power struggle, they were struck by the purposefulness of her behavior. What was infuriating before now became laughable! With good humor Mom and Dad were able to recognize the futility of Susan's behavior, as well as their own.

Guidelines for Eating Problems

1. Include children in the menu-planning process.

2. On those evenings when a meal doesn't meet the approval of a particular member, the cook will assume s/he won't be eating with the family unless informed otherwise.

3. Members choosing not to eat the prepared meal are welcome to abstain as long as they take responsibility for feeding themselves.

4. If someone has agreed to the menu and still complains, s/he may be asked to leave the table or the plate may be removed.

5. Allow children to serve themselves.

6. Don't fight with children about choice of food.

7. Never prepare special or additional food.

TABLE SQUABBLES

Once everyone is seated at the table, we usually breathe a sigh of relief and turn to our mates for our own emotional sustenance. As we become immersed in one another, we are vaguely aware of a din building steadily in the background. Then, as if awakened from a pleasant dream, we are wrenched into consciousness by the sight of a pat of butter sliding down our daughter's forehead. Instinctively, we react as if we had been dropped into the middle of a fire fight. We thrust and parry, identify the victim and culprit, and then pass sentence, judgment, and blame. "John, you have the manners of an animal. What's wrong with you anyway!" Meanwhile, Janie's crying seems to be less than authentic and we notice a rather coy grin on her face. We have a nagging feeling we've been had.

What we're witnessing is another variation on a recurring theme. Children need emotional attention, affection, and recognition just as we do. At the day's end, when most of us are in need of this emotional transfusion, we have a difficult time turning our thoughts outward. The toils of the day often make it difficult at best to attend to the needs of others. This is particularly true if you are single-parenting. However, it is at this point in the day that adults need to force themselves to attend to the needs of their children.

When forks become catapults, it's because children are feeling left out. Salad fork catapults and butter knife lances are really not weapons that children use against one another, but squad tactics designed to command and defeat unsuspecting adults. Battle lines are drawn by children and responded to by adults. Parents rush to the front attempting to mend alliances and form truces among the struggling factions without recognizing the conspiracy to get their attention. The troops do not fight against one another, but with one another against a common opponent—their parents. Indeed, most childhood fighting is designed to pull adults into their service or to overpower them.

Fighting among siblings, particularly at the dinner table, is almost always designed to command attention, service, and power in the situation. Overlooking the conspiracy involved in this misbehavior leads us to useless disciplinary tactics. Singling out one child in a fight most often does injustice to both. One is blamed, punished, and humiliated and the other is rescued, pampered, and has his/her inadequacies confirmed.

Since squabbling and clowning at the dinner table are always cooperative, these clandestine conspiracies ought to be dealt with accordingly. Fortuitously, mealtimes offer many logical and natural consequences. Fighting indicates that children are more interested in attention than eating. Therefore, both (or all) children involved can be asked to leave the table. In addition, their entourage, that is the audience which might be laughing at the behavior, can also be asked to leave. Secondly, the involved parties could be asked to leave and return when they are ready to eat instead of fight. Third, since their behavior seems to indicate that they are finished eating, although they may want our company, we may simply remove their plates. Fourth, if adults prefer, they can remove themselves. Catching children by surprise often has dramatic impact. When parents do this, children are left huffing and puffing in frustration because the adult sails have been taken out of their wind. Every strategy mentioned meets the criteria for good logical consequences. In every instance the youngster can choose for him/herself whether to stay at the table, cooperate, and eat or not eat at all. In the end, the natural consequence—hunger—ought to be allowed to run its course.

IT'S A HARD KNOCK LIFE: CHORES

In the old days, as it was noted earlier, when children overlooked their chores, the whole family experienced the consequences of their negligence. With our mechanized society today, it is generally more difficult to distribute work within the family so that children's tasks have a real effect on everyone. Meals provide a rare opportunity for children to make contributions that matter. However, if parents hope to stress responsibility, they have to be willing to put up with temporary inconvenience. For every dinnertime chore there are usually powerful logical consequences which can be brought to bear. Unfortunately, or perhaps fortunately, these logical consequences will also have an impact on the rest of the family. Therefore, in order to implement them, parents have to have a democratic, or at least consensual agreement to implement the consequences.

Setting the table, clearing the table, pouring the drinks, scraping the plates, washing the dishes, and returning the dishes to the cupboard—all are mealtime chores that can be tied to consequences, providing family members can put up with temporary inconveniences. However, these jobs should not be arbitrarily and autocratically assigned to particular family members, rather they should be chosen by family members from a list of jobs that are available.

How families choose is unimportant, as long as all members have equal access to jobs. Some families use a rotation system, drawing, etc. When possible, children should be included in preparing the job list. If the job list has been generated democratically, it is far more likely to meet with success.

Once having generated the job list, the family can also generate the consequences for those jobs in the same democratic fashion. By doing this, children have a sense of power in the situation and they are far less likely to rebel against jobs and chores which have to be done.

You'll discover that children generate very logical and democratic consequences. Children actually get compulsive once they recognize adults will be accountable to the same standards and expectations. If Dad forgets to set the table, the same rule ought to apply to him as well as the youngsters.

Let's look at one mealtime chore—table setting—for illustration. Setting the table is quite easily resolved if children are allowed to identify the logical consequences of not setting it. That is, until the table is set the family can't begin to eat. Once this basic fact is determined, a set of conditions or alternatives can be generated to meet each family's individual situation.

Some families are willing to wait, or hold dinner, until the person responsible has fulfilled his/her obligations. Other families refuse to have everyone inconvenienced as a result of one person's failure. Still others decide that each person will set his/her own place and in this way avoid hassles about setting the table. The latter recommendation is not strongly recommended since it tends to erode the spirit of cooperation.

It's important not to dock allowances or levy fines to induce compliance; it's far better to use logical consequences instead. On one hand, children ought to learn to meet their responsibilities as a result of their need to cooperate and be a member of the family. On the other hand, children are entitled to a certain amount of money because they are family members. Allowances are effective means of teaching financial responsibility. However, money shouldn't be used to discipline! This issue will be addressed later in the book. The principle applied above can be generalized to most issues surrounding mealtime chores.

It is difficult to plan, prepare, or serve a meal without clean dishes or pots and pans. Thus, anyone responsible for cooking need not do so if the kitchen is cluttered with dirty dishes. But family members need not put their backs to the wall, so to speak, by forcing this ultimatum. Intermediate alternatives are always available. For example, the following suggestions were all made by children:

1. Each person must clear his/her own plate, wash it off and place it in the dishwasher or the sink.

2. People may not be excused from the kitchen until they have taken their dishes to the sink.

3. A person may not engage in any recreation until his/her chores are done.

4. Each family member assumes a particular task in the dishwashing scheme when the entire family does them together.

These are just a few of the alternatives generated by kids. Another idea for family meals involves the job of server (hopper). The hopper is responsible for getting all those things that need to be passed and poured during the meal. Typically, Mom is left with this responsibility.

Unfortunately, this not only establishes an autocratic, but a sex-role stereotype. If the hopper is rotated among family members these stereotypes may be eliminated. Children initially take delight in seeing Dad function as the hopper or cook. Most importantly, the tone is set for a more cooperative and efficient family.

Summary

Mealtime doesn't have to be cause for a nervous breakdown. Logical consequences and encouragement can improve the cooperation and responsibility of everyone. Children must learn that services, like meals and laundry, are not provided magically. To teach this, parents must resign as maids and butlers. Temporary inconvenience quickly gives way to improved cooperation, responsibility, and genuine concern for others. A critical lesson can be learned through simple household chores. It is what Alfred Adler called "social interest." Social interest is, in the end, the recognition that others must be taken into account prior to acting on one's thoughts, desires, and emotions. Planting the seed of the true meaning of life can begin at mealtime, because through chores, children can be imbued with the glow of good feelings that comes from helping others.

12
SIBLING WARFARE AND PARENTAL COUNTERINSURGENCY

Remember, parenting is easy—until you have children.
—Anonymous, as quoted by Dolores Curran
Stress and the Healthy Family

PURPOSEFUL BEHAVIOR

When children are fighting, parents feel like they're the ones who are being put through the wringer! That's because the children's primary goal is to control us and not one another. Bill and John, ages thirteen and fourteen, lived with their mother who was recently divorced after nineteen years of marriage. Mother was just starting a new job and the boys a new school. They had just moved into a new duplex, and it seemed as though every time the three of them walked in the door a major fight broke out. When the boys' father was around, they didn't fight. After a month in the duplex, the boys had managed to break a closet door, a lamp, a stair rail, and a lounge chair.

The episode which finally brought Mom to the family counseling center occurred one Sunday evening after the boys had returned from a weekend with their father. As Mother was finishing the supper dishes, there was an explosion in the front room. "Mom, Mom, he's trying to kill me!" Knowing how violent they could get, she ran in to see the older boy (John) standing over the younger with an ax in his hands. "My God, what are you doing? Have you gone mad? Put that down now!" whereupon John stepped gallantly aside and promptly put the ax through his brother's model airplane. "That was outrageous! Get to your room right now and don't come out until tomorrow. You're going to have to pay for this, and I don't mean maybe!" After consoling the younger boy Bill and assuring him that the B-17 would be replaced, she discovered that he had earlier dumped the contents of John's favorite tackle box into the toilet and flushed it. Mother was beside herself.

This episode prompted her to come to the counseling center for help. She had spent the last two weeks policing the boys and was afraid to leave them alone fearing they might seriously injure each other. Time after time, she would find herself pulling them apart, listening to their grievances, trying to determine the culprit and then passing sentence on the villian and exonerating the victim. As the battles grew, it became impossible to tell who was the victim and who was the persecutor. Mother felt torn by their battles and began to question her ability as a parent even though prior to the divorce, she felt she had handled the boys without help from her husband. She had reached a point where most of her time was spent refereeing, judging, and sentencing the boys. Parents can find themselves playing these roles without having a license to do any of them.

Mom was unable to see any purpose in their behavior other than killing one another and driving her mad; but she knew she was spending an inordinate amount of time attending to them, being defeated by them, and feeling generally out of control. We asked her to chart the number of hours she spent policing, and all of us were amazed at the time the boys consumed. When queried about how she felt, she said, "Exhausted." Exhaustion is the fallout from attention-getting mechanisms the size of nuclear explosions—like this one. Bill and John, feeling as insecure as she, were making a megaton bid for attention and service.

Fighting usually produces knee-jerk reflexes on the part of adults. It's as if the youngsters had an invisible cord around the parents' neck and were jerking it whenever they felt a need for attention. The attention may be negative, but negative attention is much better than no attention at all. Obviously, Mother's energy and time for the boys were greatly reduced from the pre-divorce era, and the boys were making their bid for their customary share. But, what had been customary was never reasonable and now was physically impossible. The bottom line, though, was that unintentionally Mother was providing tremendous payoffs for their attention-getting conduct.

As parents, we make erroneous assumptions about fighting. We jump to the defense of the underdog because of age or sex differences, thinking that one youngster will overpower the other. Slowly we begin to realize that one child is rarely at fault or capable of an overwhelming advantage. Even when there are four or more years difference in age, the smaller child has a way of exerting power in the situation.

Further, by assuming the role of rescuer, we send mistaken messages to each child. To the oldest mischief-maker we say by word and deed, "You are a bad kid and require the supervision of an adult at all times." To the youngest or helpless ones we say, "You are not big enough or competent enough to handle your own difficulties." The helpless ones learn that they are entitled to and need secret service protection because they are incapable of protecting themselves. Both messages are discouraging.

OUR RIGHTS AND THEIRS

Generally children like fighting. That comes as quite a surprise to most parents. However, when asked by counselors or some other neutral party, most kids will be able to voice their pleasure in fighting. On the whole, parents misinterpret the purpose of fighting. When kids tell us what fun it is to fight, we have the seeds for change. Since fighting is fun or entertaining, kids ought to be able to do it, but adults shouldn't have to put up with it. Furthermore, parents shouldn't be obligated to referee. Parents ought to be able to stay out of it and not have to listen to it. Given these ground rules, there are some general, solid guidelines that can be followed. Within this framework each family will have to tailor specific strategies.

Let Them Fight

At a neutral time, negotiate an agreement with the kids. Give them the good news first. They are welcome to fight as long as they like, and you will no longer interfere. Even better, you aren't going to nag them about getting along or bickering. Now, the bad news. From this day forward, regardless of how bloody the encounter, you no longer will intervene on anyone's behalf. Further, since it is fair for them to fight, it's fair that the adults should not have to listen to it. Therefore, they may choose a spot outside the house where they can fight, rain or shine, warm or cold. When the children are allowed to take the initiative for finding a suitable place, they usually come up with the garage or alley; both spots are serviceable.

Merely choosing a place to fight will not stop altercations because the kids will test your commitment to the new strategies. Therefore, parents must say that if any bickering, fighting, or shouting occurs, they will simply say, "I see you have decided to go to the garage." With the choice offered, the youngsters have the option of removing themselves or stopping the fight. If the disturbance continues, the next choice is provided. "You may go by yourself or I will take you." Once this choice has been provided and the children fail to move, the adult quietly and firmly moves one of the children to the garage. If the agreement has been struck with the kids prior to the fight, they usually will comply without having to be taken by force. This was done with Bill and John, and it proved very effective.

In those instances when children are too big to be removed, the best alternative is to remove yourself. Preferably, the adult should vacate and get far enough away to avoid hearing the fallout or caring about the neighbors' reaction. Since the kids' behavior started with a powerful bid for attention, the attention they seek must be provided in a useful way. Without encouragement the misbehavior will return regardless of the discipline employed. Special time should be scheduled for each child. Deeply discouraged kids may refuse special time at first, but eventually they will try it. Once youngsters become accustomed to special time, their fighting will diminish. Research demonstrates, in the case of fighting, that special time alone can reduce the incidence (Kelly and Main, 1979.)

Special Circumstances

Fighting doesn't always occur at home. It can occur when you are virtually held captive by the battlers. Driving in the car is usually one of these vulnerable times. Somehow kids know when you're vulnerable. While you're held captive by traffic or schedules, they joyously pommel each other in the back seat.

Perhaps you're on the way home from the market when the children start in. You nag and half-heartedly try to separate them as they bounce around in the back seat. Stopping for a red light, you make a lightning attack but are pulled up short as the light changes and the driver of the Greyhound bus behind you blasts his horn.

Finally you see your chance. There is an unusually long line of traffic at the next light which may give you an opportunity to join in the kids' fight. Traffic is stopped, and you stretch over the back seat with one foot on the brake, your back arched, and one hand on the wheel. You swat wildly, but your blow lands with an unsatisfying pat. In uncontrolled rage, you scream clenched-teeth obscenities just as the school principal pulls alongside. Your guilt is intensified as the principal follows you. Eventually, he turns off—but the next week, every time the phone rings, you're sure it's the committe on child abuse.

What to Do?

The most effective tactic for dealing with automobile anarchy may cause some inconvenience, but will save you time and headaches in the long run. As soon as it's safe, pull over to the side of the road and ask the children to step into the ditch or onto the sidewalk. There they are welcome to fight it out and return to the car when they are finished. It's better to initiate this technique for the first time when you're going to Disney World or to another place where the kids want to go. This strategy is simple and effective. An alternative for school bus drivers as well as parents is to stop the vehicle, remove the keys, and step into the ditch yourself. Depending upon the weather and your destination, this can be very effective. For school bus drivers on the way home from school, this is absolute magic. Parents also like this method if the children are older/bigger and a little too bulky to drag out of the back seat.

Children's behavior on the school bus illustrates what will most often happen when children are fighting and adults make their exit. In many cases, some kids may be passive observers or victims of the disturbance. At first, this may seem terribly unfair; but the victims and observers may be supporting the behavior by not assuming their civic responsibility or by laughing at, or fighting with, the instigators. When group pressure is brought to bear, the adults are relieved of their responsibilities as policemen. Children will always elect adults as policemen if adults allow them to. When bus behavior is too severe to be dealt with by using these logical consequences, then the privilege, not the right, of riding the bus should be suspended.

In a Crowd

Public places—supermarkets, churches, and the homes of others—can give children opportunities for tyranny. In these situations, the first option for adults is to remove themselves if possible. When adults evacuate the arena, the children will usually be left to experience the embarrassment of their actions. But, if their behavior infringes upon the rights of others, then kids should be treated like a New Year's resolution—and carried out. Once out of the public view, the youngster should be taken home and left, if old enough, or taken to a prearranged sitter. Children need to know in advance the consequences for misbehavior. When they do, they may test the situation at first; however, they will stop on their own if they know follow-through is inevitable.

COPING WITH COUNTERINSURGENCY

In the opening scenario, Bill, John, and Mother were able to implement the strategies successfully. Interestingly, John refused special time for almost four weeks; then he cashed in. Almost instantly, there was a dramatic decline in the incidence of fighting. Not long after, the logical consequences discussed earlier were employed, and the fighting disappeared.

Initially, the boys were anxious to see if Mother really intended to let them fight. "I see you have decided to go to the garage," Mom said. "Yeah, let's go, John. This time Mom's not going to butt in and save you." Off they went, eager to test themselves and Mother. Once in the garage, the noise quickly subsided. On one occasion Mother couldn't bear the suspense, and she crept cautiously to the back door and glanced into the garage. There, circling and retreating steadily was, of all people, John. Not long after, they both returned to the house with John muttering something about Bill fighting like a girl. Mother paid no attention, and the boys went to their rooms. That evening was surprisingly uneventful.

A few weeks later, a loud disagreement developed, so Mother grabbed her coat, obviously preparing to leave the house. John, the older boy, blurted loudly, "Mom, one of us is really going to get hurt if you let this go on." "Exactly," Mother responded, as she walked out the door. Children, regardless of their age, recognize they have the power to choose between getting hurt and working out mutually acceptable solutions to their disagreements. This places children in a paradoxical bind that encourages responsibility. On the one hand, they can fight if they like and experience the unabashed consequences of their actions, or they can cooperate. In either case, they are forced to assume responsibility.

Guidelines for Sibling Warfare

1. At a neutral time notify the youngsters that they are old enough to handle their own disagreements, and that you will no longer nag, judge, or rescue anyone.

2. Locate a place for fighting that is agreeable to everyone.

3. Remove the children or yourself without talking.

4. Offer special time unconditionally.

5. Stick to your guns!

13

BOWEL, BLADDER, OVARIES, AND TESTES: Handling the Power Tools

Control the situation, not the child.

—*F*.*M*.

This chapter is essentially the Black and Decker manual for handling power tools. The toughest problems parents face today involve physiological power—bowel, bladder, ovaries, testes, and brain. These are the *quid pro quos* of kids. An eye for an eye—or power for power. When kids are too young to make sense of their emotions, they often respond with "organ dialect," to use Adler's phrase. Adults can use it too. In fact within some families a particular organ or physical problem often does the talking: colitis, ulcers, arthritis, asthma, etc.

Black and Decker exchanges, as the name implies, are a balanced trade of some kind. When kids employ sleeplessness, elimination, starvation, or their reproductive organs to defeat others, they are exchanging power for power. The more dependent adults have become on personal power in their disciplinary style, the earlier these organ power tools will be used by children.

A recurring theme of this book is power vs. powerlessness. As Walter O'Connell noted, all people need and get power. The language of power and powerlessness is spoken across every life task and in every language of the body. Children discover, long before parents do, that their organs cannot be controlled by anyone. When adults try to usurp children's brains and bodies, children exchange power for power.

CONTROLLING CONSCIOUSNESS

When children are very young, parents try to control their consciousness in such matters from the trivial such as sleep to the monumental, such as whom to love. When it comes to inducing sleep, parents will try the most amazing methods. For instance, they step into a child's room at 9:15 and command, "Get to sleep right now!" And of course, the youngster lapses into a coma—right? If the child doesn't, the parents might ask themselves "When was the last time I fell asleep on command?" The answer to that question may help parents understand the crazy expectations they try to impose on their children's consciousness.

One mother complained bitterly that her eight-year-old son would crawl under the covers after she had turned out the lights and read late into the night. Mom said he usually fell asleep reading. In cases like this, the problem is the parent's, not the child's. Mother worried needlessly. "Is the boy getting up in the morning?" I asked. "Oh, sure, but he refuses to go to sleep when I turn out the light." I suggested that if this boy was old enough to read, he was probably old enough to turn off his own light. She was certain the boy would read until dawn. Luckily, as soon as the boy was given control of his own light and consciousness, he fell asleep.

The principle here is simple: Don't struggle with another person's mind; you can't win. Eight-year-olds reading Melville don't need an adult's help to turn out the light or decide when they're tired. Few, if any, children need help deciding when they are tired. All of us have experienced the youngster who literally fights sleep. Yet, the battle isn't won when adults step into their room and yell, "Sleep!" Nothing like a good 80-decibel yell to settle a youngster down.

Parents need to wake up and try letting children make adjustments in their own schedules. Morning does come, and with it come the responsibilities of the day. Therefore, children should be held accountable for all their morning responsibilities. The natural consequence, exhaustion, aids in the training process. Children learn quickly that they feel better and can do more the next day if they sleep. The battle isn't won by force and isn't fought over whether or not they should sleep. The contest is over control or power.

Guidelines for Lights Out

1. Diagnose the problem by judging your emotional reacton. If

you feel anger, you feel your power challenged. Your frustration signals a bid for service and attention.

2. Don't act as if turning out the lights will control your child's consciousness.

3. Allow the natural consequences (fatigue) and the logical consequences (daily responsibilities) to act as disciplinarians.

DO YOU HAVE TO GO TINKY?

Trying to assume responsibility for a child's bowel and bladder is probably the most fickle and discouraging thing a parent can do. As parents, we become very "hyper" about youngsters' elimination processes when they approach that age when they're "supposed to be trained." Usually bowel and bladder problems develop for two reasons. First, parents begin training too early and are too intense about the youngster's lack of progress. Secondly, occasionally there are legitimate physical problems involving constricted urethras, most frequent in little girls, and insufficient bladder size in little boys. A thorough physical examination will determine whether there are any physical difficulties, and then you can deal with these concerns.

Trying to assume responsibility for another person's physiology is ridiculous, but just *how* ridiculous is difficult to grasp until we reflect on our behavior as we're about to take a twenty-minute cross town jaunt with our kids.

We have everyone file into formation for inspection. "Does anyone have to go to the bathroom before we leave? We're not stopping. Katie, I don't care if you don't have to go. Try to get a little out anyway." What's wrong with that, you ask? Katie's eleven! One would think that an eleven-year-old would know if her bladder was full or not; but Dad doesn't take no for an answer and presses the issue by calling Katie a liar or stupid. Dad assumes that Katie isn't smart enough to figure out whether her own bladder needs to be emptied.

Parents often shadow children to avoid accidents. "Jimmy, why don't you go potty before you watch Sesame Street?" or "Why don't you try to get a little out before you eat?" And, the best of all, "Why don't you go potty for Daddy before you take your nap?" Talk about clever ways to confuse a three-year-old who's trying his best to control

157

his own functions. Is he supposed to go for Mom too? In response to this plea, one struggling three-year-old said, "Mommy, I gotta go for me first."

Bed-wetting

Of course, bedtime can really intensify these struggles with the "power tools." Bed-wetting is not a real problem until the child is five or six years old. The tactics suggested now are for youngsters four and older. First, get out of the business of policing the child's nighttime routine. Don't talk to children about drinking or wetting the bed. (The suggestion may cause the problem.) Second, don't allow youngsters to sleep with you or siblings if they wet the bed during the night. Third, when they do wet the bed, have them strip their own bed and take the soiled bedding to the wash room. Fourth, depending upon the age of the child, they should be encouraged to remake their own bed or sleep in what remains unsoiled. Clean bedclothes should be moved to a place where the child can have access to them. Finally, the parents' attitude should be, in behavior and spirit, "You can handle it." Don't chide, moralize, belittle, or discipline the youngster. Assume that he or she can and will handle it.

Bowel Control

"Mike, tell Mommy the truth. Did you go stinky in your pants?" This usually doesn't require a confession. You don't want an indictment; you want a diaper. The situation doesn't require or deserve a confession or moralizing. When moral castigation fails, we resort to idle threats. "If you don't stop going acky in your pants, Santa Claus is going to bring you a stick and a piece of coal for Christmas." The kid thinks coal is a precious metal and isn't sure what s/he is supposed to do with the stick. "You're not going to ruin my bridge party by smelling up the living room. You're going to go if I have to sit here with you all day." The epitaph to this threat is that parents sit in the bathroom half the day, are miserably prepared for the bridge party, and the kid stinks up the living room so badly during the second hand that he wilts all the flowers in the room.

Three- and four-year-olds are old enough to decide if their pants need changing. Further, they are probably capable of changing and rinsing them. There is always a chance that youngsters will choose to wear dirty pants. If that happens, the choice is theirs; but where they sit and play becomes your choice. Cleaning up after themselves is novel and encouraging, but gets old fast. Parents may have to supervise and help in the clean-up but it should be done after the child has made his/her best attempt.

Guidelines for Handling Power Tools

1. Bowel and bladder control are just problems of control in general.

2. Don't attempt to control what you can't.

3. Avoid trying to train children too young; youngsters will let you know when it's time.

4. Turn bowel and bladder control issues over to the children.

5. Avoid unnecessary comments.

6. Allow the children to clean up their own messes.

7. Teach children how to change their own bed linen.

8. Don't moralize.

REPRODUCTION AND SEDUCTION

Seduction and reproduction bring us closer to hypocrisy than any other issues in parenting. We are hypocritical on several counts. First, when our sons leave the house in the evening, our sexual advice ranges from "have a good time" to the coy line, "Don't do anything I wouldn't do!" On the other hand, when our daughters depart, our counsel includes rape prevention strategies and a folksy story about Mom and Dad still being celibate two years after marriage.

Unfortunately, we go beyond story-telling under pressure and begin to launch edicts. "You'll have premarital sex over my dead body." In response to this ultimatum, you are likely to find birth control pills in your daughter's lunch box along with the Twinkies. Edicts are also great material for destroying adult-child relationships during adolescence. "We forbid you to see him/her ever again." This statement is guaranteed to work wonders! It's been known to turn lukewarm romances into passionate affairs. Pointing out the foibles, ineptitudes, and dim-wittedness of your child's friend will likely succeed in cementing what may have been a very mediocre romance. Nothing will bring these two people together more quickly than a common enemy—you. Young couples, convinced of injustice, will find music, poetry, and art that symbolizes their struggle against you. So, if you want to cement what only God should, forbid them to see one another!

The love of an adolescent is held in an open hand, not a closed fist! Therefore, do the unexpected and paradoxical thing: open your house and home to the potential in-law and act accordingly. Invite the boy or girlfriend to traditional family outings that have long been valued by everyone. Allow the new love's behavior to speak for itself. If the friend finds a family tradition dumb, his/her behavior will speak more loudly than you ever could. Extend the invitation to include special meals and occasions. Only in these situations will your child be able to tell if the new love values what s/he values.

Provide constructive ways in which the young people can learn about each other's values, goals, and aspirations. This can be done by including church. The old invitation-to-church trick will discourage more superficially intended and marginally principled individuals than any ultimatum. This never fails. That is not to say that in every case it has driven the friend off; the opposite has also occurred. The new friend sometimes becomes a welcome addition to the family, because parents have grown to know, understand, and appreciate the young person as their child has.

The genuineness of any relationship cannot be tested in the midst of adult-child conflict. Have the courage to allow your youngsters to freely formulate their impressions of people. Be encouraging; say in word and deed, "We trust and respect your judgment about people. This person must be pretty special."

The proverbial bottom line in this issue is sex and unwanted pregnancy. For teenagers in the process of becoming adults, responsible behavior and encouragement must begin early. The important thing is to talk openly and directly to children about sexuality and values.

Your own attitude toward sex, as well as your openness and comfort with your own sexuality, will be monitored carefully by your children.

Mothers can model early attitudes about sexuality by the way they handle their own menstruation. Parents ought to be open about their personal hygiene and Mother ought to be open about her menstruation and her choice of hygiene, tampons, pads, etc. This attitude of openness can carry over into issues of sexuality which will become so important later on.

Parents often wonder "How much do I tell them?" A good barometer is a very simple one: give children the information they ask for, but don't bore them. Kids tend to need bits and pieces of information as questions arise. Provide the basic information but don't deliver a biology lecture and lesson in morality when the kids ask what it means to "go all the way."

Open the doors of communication about sexuality at an early age—five isn't too young. Listen carefully to determine if the child is asking for information or reassurance and emotional support. As kids get older, they seek support for their behavior by asking vague questions about sexuality. Don't tell them how many sperm are in a drop of semen if what they really want to know is whether they're entitled to conflicting emotions like, "I want to, but I don't want to."

Knowing what's being asked of you as a parent is probably the toughest assignment. When in doubt, don't smother the child with information—just listen. Reflect or paraphrase feelings by using the active listening skills talked about in chapter five. For example, a conversation with your teenage daughter might contain reflective comments like these: "Your body is saying one thing, but your heart is telling you another." Or "You want his love very badly but you're not sure having sex is going to get it."

As you try to help children learn to cope with their sexuality the four basic components of democratic communication discussed in chapter five become critical:

1. Seek meaning
2. Voice observations
3. Give support
4. Seek alternatives

Because of the heightened awareness of sexuality in society today, children are confronted with choices you never had to make at their age. Just remember you did make the same decisions, you probably just made them a little later in life and under less pressure. Don't give kids solutions to problems they don't have. Remember what's needed in issues of reproduction and seduction is a little information and a lot of support. Make an effort to distinguish between the content and emotional messages between you and your child.

Guidelines for Handling Young Love Affairs

1. Don't try to "forbid" anything; make requests and not demands.
2. Open your home and heart to new friends.
3. Compliment children on their selection of friends and find assets, not faults.
4. Deal with sexuality and birth control early and openly.

Summary

Parental threats and ultimatums are no match for the child's power tools. The child's physical system is beyond your control. Nevertheless, you need not support any discouraged uncooperative behavior whether it's bed-wetting or promiscuity. In either instance, youngsters will have to experience the full weight of their carelessness; a parent's task is to make sure they're prepared and capable of choosing well.

The "big guns" are best handled through the natural consequences of the social order. Attempting punitive, unilateral moral decrees will only meet with defeat. Every strategy suggested above is based on the principles of logical consequences and the knowledge that we are no more capable of controlling our children's physiology than we are of controlling our mate's.

14
THE GRIMMYS:
Awards of Martyrdom
and Other Special Effects

All people need and get power.
—Walter O'Connell

Her father loved the children intensely. When they were young, he was their joyful playmate, but as they grew older he became a possessive, controlling tyrant. According to biographer Isabel Clark, Ba once said of her father,

> What you do not see, what you cannot see, is the deep tender affection behind and below all those patriarchal ideas of governing grown-up children in the way they must go... The evil is in the system—and he simply takes it to his own views of the propriety of happiness—he takes it to be his duty to rule like the kings of Christendom, by divine right.

"Ba," as her family called her, (short for Baby) was the eldest, his favorite, and the most gifted. At the age of thirteen, she became mysteriously ill and so frail that her family felt surely she would die as a young spinster. Quite miraculously, she left her invalid bed at the age of thirty-eight to get married. Her sickness became her "identity" card and was so entrenched in the family system that the physical configuration of the house as well as sibling relationships revolved around her infirmity. The family portrayed themselves as generous, self-sacrificing protectors while maintaining oppressive control under the cloak of concern. Mother was strangely a peripheral figure, flitting through Ba's life. She died when Ba was twenty-two, apparently unsung or wept.

Although rigidly controlled, Ba exercised her freedom in two ways—with her writing and her diet. According to Clark, her father complained that "obstinacy and a diet of dry toast kept her ill." Her suitor, Robert, first grew to know and love her through her writing. When they first met, she was well on her way to becoming a spinster at thirty-eight. She looked much younger than her years due to her frail physique at 5 feet tall and 87 pounds. Eventually Robert coaxed her from her invalid bed into his life. Ba said of her love for Robert, "I yield the grave for thy sake, and exchange my near sweet view of heaven for earth for thee."

To avoid her father's wrath, they eloped in secrecy and began their life together in a different country. Her father disowned her and went to his grave calloused and unrelenting. Although Ba's health improved miraculously through the early years of marriage and the couple was blessed with a son, the loss of her father's affection plagued her.

Such was the captivating life and art of Elizabeth Barrett Browning. The "Sonnets from the Portuguese" lucidly describe the nobility of her suffering and the sacrifices required in giving up that nobility. According to psychologist Carol Lewis, Browning's mysterious affliction has been diagnosed as anorexia. But the broader picture could focus on Ba's "identity" as sufferer. One of her few poems absent of melancholy was her last. In truth, her "near sweet view of heaven" was maintained by a hypersensitivity to life. Characteristically, her view of life contributed to chronic bouts of depression which triggered, or were accompanied by, chronic respiratory and eating difficulties.

Suffering and martyrdom become the "identity" card for many of us from time to time. This self-inflicted moroseness is one of the most potent useless goals. When youngsters are overpowered, constricted, and punished for their instinctive need to be independent and autonomous, they may inflict revenge upon those who imprison them through their own suffering.

Nothing hurts or manipulates parents more than the suffering of their children or spouses. Every family member knows on some level that the sufferer uses self-sacrifice and helplessness and this has the paradoxical effect of overpowering everyone. In order to stay in her father's cage, Ba had to suffer and swing on death's door. She transmitted a message to her father and perhaps the world, "You can make me live in your pretty cage...but you cannot make me live." Most people don't transform suffering into literary classics as Ba did, but most martyrs elevate their sense of nobility a little.

Martyrdom can achieve the useless goals of power/control and revenge. "I thought power and revenge were different," you say. Correct! The useless goals of power and revenge are different in their ends, but are often similar in their means—suffering. Martyrdom utilizes self-sacrifice (internalized hurt and self-destruction) as the prime method of moving others.

Anorexia, depression, and certain psychosomatic problems—all self-inflicted disorders—are soul mates cultivated during early family life. Such suffering threatens actual or emotional loss. Suffering therefore has the potential to control others and/or to prevent others from controlling. Failing to do either, the sufferer determines to make "them" pay. The runaway, for example, always has reveries about the ways in which "they'll be sorry."

Sullenness, seething rage, and suffering are common to depression and eating disorders. Recently, Dr. Timothy Walsh reported that a kind of blood test (dexamethasone suppression) used to assess depression has generated similar metabolic results among anorexics. What's noteworthy here are the metabolic as well as psychological similarities between depression and eating disorders. The psychological similarity seems to be in the goal-directed nature of the symptoms. Anorexics and depressives unconsciously want to exert as much control over others as others have exerted over them.

Although behaviors due to depression or eating disorders are imposing, the patterns begin at a much earlier age, when the child's hypersensitivity is more transparent and less awesome. Consider the story of Brad.

Brad, a middle child, had just celebrated his fifth birthday. In five short years, he had developed a keen eye for injustice. One late summer day, as a result of what he felt was a stinging injustice at the hands of his parents, he decided to run away. He shuffled silently from his room, suitcase in hand and knapsack on his back. Dad, who was busily fixing the kitchen sink, was genuinely shaken by Brad's sullen and sorrowful appearance.

"Where are you going?"

"I'm leaving!"

"How far do you think you'll get? You don't have any money. Where will you stay?"

"I'll get a job at the fair."

Dad's attempts to reason with the five-year-old failed. Mother overheard and sensed Dad's guilt and confusion. She thoughtfully declared, "I think he should go ahead and try it on his own for awhile." Brad was noticeably off balance and so was Dad. Brad, now whining loudly, bid a slow good-bye to the pets as he fixed himself a PBJ for the trail. Having milked the moment for all the parental guilt possible, he left.

As he trudged out of sight, Mom and Dad pressed themselves against the window to see where he was going without being detected. Half-heartedly they returned to their chores, periodically checking the window—nothing! Then, about an hour and a half later, Brad appeared. He waited outside a long time—then the doorbell rang. As casually as possible, both Mom and Dad answered the door. There stood Brad appearing mildly perturbed but not depressed. "Brad, it's good to see you back!" they said.

"Yeah," he paused, "I s'pose ya still got the same old cat, huh!" Then Brad marched past Mom and Dad to his room.

Brad sensed his actions were useless, but did not want to brush the injustice under the rug or let Mom and Dad off the hook. "S'pose you still got the same old cat" served notice beautifully. In essence, the message was "I'll let that one go for now, but don't think I accept the injustice you subject me to."

Because young children are so transparent, it's far easier to see the humor in their behavior. As kids get older, episodes become more devastating. Indeed, this category of problems—martyrdom, depression, and eating disorders—have a sobering impact on all families.

Martyrdom isn't always easy to recognize. Sometimes it's difficult for parents to recognize or accept the intentions of a child's actions, and children are only vaguely aware of their true motives. Their purpose is usually lost in the all-out desire to hurt or control the parent. The emotional side effects—hurt, pain, and guilt—are dimly envisioned by the child.

Parents also erroneously assume that the problem is the child's. However, the late psychiatrist William Pew was fond of saying, "No one's to blame but everyone's responsible." Martyrdom, like all useless behavior, is socially embedded. But, in order for martyrdom to work, the family must lift the sufferer up to be canonized. The family has to participate, actively support, and yes, even encourage suffering. According to Oscar Christensen, noted family counselor, family members who inadvertently support martyrdom become the martyr's "entourage." The words of advice to parents in this case are—don't do it! Try to avoid being a part of the sufferer's entourage.

Depressives, especially anorexics, are parent "watchers." These children, more so than most, spend inordinate amounts of time watching their parents and gauging their own behavior accordingly. And, not surprisingly, parents of anorexic and depressed children are often emotional power brokers. In Ba's case, her father was a loving but controlling tyrant. In other families an ambivalence exists between the anorexic daughter and mother—mother acts like a competitive sister rather than a mother, for instance. In still other families, parents seem to be disenfranchised, separated and aloof. For example, Dr. Joel Yager points out that among all reported bouts of anorexia, 34 percent followed explicit threats of marital separation by the father and 19 percent followed a separation threat by the mother. Thus, if parents are emotionally oppressive, threaten emotional abandonment via divorce or isolation, or create role ambivalence by competing with the child, emotions are elevated to the status of weapons in the family. In order to survive, each family member may seek to develop his or her own arsenal.

"S'pose ya got the same old cat" gives us lighthearted insight into a sobering dynamic. Even very young children can astutely use fear, sullenness, shyness, and sadness to control other people. Age itself does not predict the complexity of behavior. Both cases—Brad, the five-year-old runaway, and Ba, the thirteen-year-old anorexic—illustrate the theme of suffering as means of manipulating family relationships.

ENCOURAGING ATTITUDES

As parents of potential martyrs, the first thing you must do is to be critical of your own motives with your children. The watchwords for discipline are these: *control the situation, not the child.* Trying to control the child and demanding compliance will breed subversive rebellion among martyrs and depressives.

Second, while you may recognize the manipulative quality of martyrdom, you should not underestimate the sincerity of the self-destructiveness.

Third, parents must be conscious of alliances that are inappropriately built between parents and children or between other siblings. For example, if the mother has casually confided in a daughter concerning a problem in her relationship with Dad, the daughter, if a martyr, may assume emotional responsibility for solving the discord.

Fourth, when you have more invested in the child's happiness than the child does, you will be sucked into an emotional sting. Brad's parents made a very loving and responsible decision. They talked and acted as if they loved him deeply, but were not in control of his happiness. As an example, they said, "I think he ought to try it on his own awhile." For other parents it may be, "We care about you deeply, but we cannot keep you alive. Only you can do that." Or "If you continue to abuse drugs, you cannot live with us. Would you be willing to move to an inpatient facility?" These statements demonstrate ways for parents to indicate that they are exercising less responsibility for the child's happiness *and* that the child should assume more.

Fifth, to the extent that it is possible, parents should encourage the child by providing special service and attention on the useful side of life. Allow the child to succeed and fail.

Finally, the "entourage" must be minimized. The child wants to draw as many people as possible into his or her service. If you need professional help, coordinate your efforts through one professional. The sufferer incorporates others into his/her entourage in an egocentric, self-centered way. This lack of other-directedness is a hallmark of the martyr.

Guidelines for Discouraging Martyrdom

1. Be critical of your own motives with your children. Strive to control yourself and not the child.

2. Don't make inappropriate family alliances. You can love your children but you will always be their parent, never their buddy.

3. Avoid investing more in your child's behavior than your child does.

4. Be legitimately encouraging.

5. Treat suffering as a friendly warning and as a protective device. Pouty, sullen behavior may signal the fact that you are assuming too much of the child's responsibility.

6. Don't discount the child's emotions by dishing out emotional cookies, like "Oh that's all right. Have a snack—you'll feel better tomorrow."

7. Do the unexpected. Instead of fighting with the symptom (trying to make the child happy) suggest that the child may want to take his/her time getting over the blow. After all, what happened was very important to the child and s/he is entitled to be gloomy.

Summary

Although you may need professional help redirecting the self-sacrificing behavior of a child, there are steps that you can take to avoid martyrdom. The most important of these is to accept the fact that all behavior takes place in a social context. Martyrdom is merely a symptom that something is wrong in your family. You may want the child to eat, be less depressed, etc., without changing the way the family works. However, if you want the martyr to give up his/her "saintly status," the family is going to have to change and perhaps be temporarily inconvenienced.

Parents as absolute rulers can be buried by a powerless depressive. Critical, belittling, insensitive parents can be sensitized through a hypersensitive child.

Therefore, to avoid martyrdom, look long and hard at the suffering of your children to see if it doesn't mirror the opposite of your own extremes: powerlessness vs. tyranny, insensitivity vs. hypersensitivity, and absolute ruler/controller vs. the uncontrollable. Then, instead of demanding that others change, first ask how *you* can.

15

WAGE AND SALARY DISPUTES: Allowances

Affluence itself is not offensive, but the irrespon-
sibility it can create is.

—F.M.

BUYING TROUBLE

There is no better way to buy poor behavior from children than by trying to pay them for being good. Once children make the connection between your need for peace and your willingness to pay for it, a vicious cycle starts. Youngsters who hold their parents hostage in the supermarket check-out lane have learned this well. All of us have observed this scene:

"Mommy, I want that candy bar!"

"No, it's too close to dinner."

"I want it, I want it." Then as if the act has been rehearsed, the youngster throws himself on the floor and gives the performance of his life.

Everyone within earshot hears the blood curdling screams and assumes some parent is publicly abusing his or her child. As the child rolls and kicks on the floor, customers gather to observe the outcome. Who will win? Mother is initially defiant and refuses to give in, but as the crowd gathers she weakens and finds herself jamming her hand into her purse to buy the candy bar. She leaves disgusted with herself and vows not to give in next time. But the next time comes all too quickly, and the audience includes friends and in-laws, so Mom succumbs to the pressure more quickly than she did the last time. Parents are extorted because they believe erroneously that it's more convenient and practical to serve as banker than to let children handle their own money. "If I control the money, I'll control the child." False! Adults who support Oscar-winning performances like the struggle described above make two fatal mistakes, one involves the "givum" reflex and the other involves emotional bankruptcy.

"Givum" Reflex

The "givum" reflex is an unconscious palm slap to the pocket, followed by a handout of cash. It is a reflex because we never remember it. But children do remember! They learn that persistent obnoxious behavior will reap great rewards. And, they learn that the well never runs dry; money will always be magically provided by an external source.

Emotional Bankruptcy

Emotional bankruptcy is like a neurological tic—it's always present, but there doesn't seem to be anything you can do about it. Every time the child initiates a demand for money, you can't say no. If giving in and providing cash on demand seems easier than trying to teach your children money management skills, you're probably incurring fiscal and emotional debt. Every situation requires deliberation of weighty issues: Should Mary be given the money? Is she getting more than her sister? Is this a wise purchase? Maybe she deserves the money but shouldn't have the candy! By the time parents weigh the pros and cons they're exhausted. Then they usually hand out the money anyway, which causes frustration—and more emotional drain. Next, the child accepts the handout without gratitude. Now the parent is angry and emotionally bankrupt.

Though exhausted, parents may still claim, "But I know what's best for my child." That's probably true in many cases, but try accounting for all the things you buy for your kids. You'll discover that you buy many things for them that they would not buy for themselves—if they had the power and responsibility.

MONEY 101

There is no better way to produce fiscally irresponsible children than to prohibit them from managing their own money. Extortion plots and other kinds of fiscal irresponsibility can be eliminated if children are provided with money in a democratic way. The allowance is an excellent way to accomplish this. You may have some questions you want answered before plunging into negotiations with your children: How old should they be? How much should they get? What guidelines need to be provided for its use? Should all kids receive the same amount? and so on.

There are several guidelines for handling financial issues which should generalize to every family. Within these standards each family should be able to make its unique application. Families need to consider the following:

1. The child's financial need.
2. The financial resources of the family.
3. The child's experience with money.
4. The child's developmental ability.

These rules of thumb should answer several questions. The chronological age of the child isn't terribly significant, but the child's demonstrated need for money at a particular age *is*. Three- and four-year-olds attend birthday parties, go to Sunday school and make an offering, and find plenty to buy in the supermarket. All of these activities demonstrate the child's need to have and be responsible for money. Family resources will establish the proverbial bottom line. The youngster's experience with money should play a role in the amount dispensed.

Based on experience and need, allowances can be negotiated. Families shouldn't move directly to a full allowance in order to practice money management. (A full allowance is one in which children assume total responsibility for their personal necessities: wardrobe, school lunches, church pledges, birthday gifts, school supplies, vacation cash, car insurance, and "blow dough.") Partial or limited allowances should be offered for youngsters who are first learning to use money. As skills and needs develop, allowances can grow into a complete budget.

Limited and complete allowances raise the issue of the purpose for providing cash. If allowances are implemented for the wrong reasons they can become handouts. Money ought to be provided for only two reasons: first, money can be used to develop cash management skills and to educate the child in financial independence; and second, money should be shared because everyone deserves an amount of monetary power as a family member. Parents should discuss and negotiate the amount of cash required and identify budget items that should become the responsibility of the child. Beginning allowances can include movie money, church offerings, and the like. Once the youngster has cash in hand, "supermarket extortion" should be eliminated. When the child makes his bid for a purchase, the adult need only ask if he has brought his money along. If he hasn't, the outcome is obvious and logically consequential.

The youngster may buy the candy with his/her own money or go without. If going without means having a fit, remove yourself or the child—but don't give in. In most cases if the youngster cannot afford to buy the candy bar, that's his or her problem, not yours and the youngster knows it; the temper tantrum usually disappears.

Money introduces kids to the economic realities of life which are exciting, sobering, and educational. The child who spends his/her week's allowance on a Chinese yo-yo at the fair, only to have it break before getting home, begins to appreciate deferred gratification. This lesson, perhaps more than any other, is worth the price of a weekly allowance to parents. Today's children have little opportunity to defer gratification for any reason. Parents and grandparents provide for the child's every need, even before the child has a need. Allowances are another way of offering a youngster the opportunity to overcome adversity, a critical ingredient to successful independence.

How Much?

The pivotal question in financial training is, "How much money is enough?" The guideline is simple and appropriate for children of all ages. First, look at the needs of the child; next identify what he can provide for himself and what he cannot provide; then provide all of the latter and very little of the former.

Needs and Wants

A budget should be generated in cooperation with the child based upon two things: the child's needs and the child's wants. First, establish

174

which needs must be provided by you and which needs could be provided by the child. For example, a thirteen-year-old girl "needs" food, shelter, clothing, and an education, so it's reasonable to assume that parents of a thirteen-year-old should be responsible for these things. But, the daughter could assume responsibility for clothing if the parents included a clothing allotment in her allowance.

Secondly, there are things that may *seem* essential to the child, but are really "wants." For example, if a fourteen-year-old boy has decided to run for student council president he may feel he "needs" money for campaigning. Indeed, he will have expenses, but that's because he "wants" to be president. Expenses like this, although difficult to classify, ought to be the child's responsibility. Similarly, if an eight-year-old girl plans to fulfill a requirement for a Brownie merit badge, she may feel she needs money for supplies. In fact, she *wants* to be a Brownie and therefore, those expenses could be included in her allowance.

An effective guideline might be to provide everything children *need*, while allowing them to assume responsibility for as much as they can without disrupting their lives. And finally, provide less than what they *want*—significantly less.

Parents today, rich and poor, provide twice as much as their children will ever need or use. By estimating what your child needs and wants and then providing less, you are doing the youngster a service. An allowance should be a provision for training, not a juvenile endowment for indulgence. There should be incentive to save, work, and defer gratification. These virtues are values every child ought to have the opportunity to learn.

THE HIRED HELP

At times parents are tempted to tie children's allowances to performance of household tasks. *Don't do it!* The allowance should not be used as a means of hiring live-in domestic help. That doesn't mean that children shouldn't be expected to do household chores, only that money shouldn't be the fulcrum to induce responsibility. When was the last time you were paid for cooking a meal or doing the wash? "Have you lost your senses?" you may reply. Well, hiring your children as domestics is equally crazy.

175

Parents and spouses do for one another and their children because they are internally motivated, not because they're paid; so it should be for children. Being a family member—spouse or child—incurs a great deal of responsibility which can only be supported by internal motivation—not money. There are some exceptions; jobs that parents would hire done, such as cutting and stacking wood or digging up a hedge, can be contracted with kids. This gives children an opportunity to earn money for things they want.

TEENAGERS AS WAGE EARNERS

Once kids are old enough to work, allowances can be maintained but they should be renegotiated from time to time. When school-age kids become immersed in a "job" to maintain a car, dates, clothes or entertainment, their education suffers. For this reason alone, an allowance is valuable. All youngsters should be encouraged to work, regardless of their affluence, but the work ought to be an exercise in mental or physical discipline, not all-consuming toil that supports material indulgences.

"What's too much work?" There is no right answer to this question. Generally, college-age kids should work no more than twenty hours a week unless the work is career related. High school kids shouldn't work more than fifteen hours a week and preferably ten hours or less. If the work is career-related, exceptions can be made. The most important advice to remember is this: do not use money to try to control your children. They quickly discover the ideal way to break out of your financial control—a full-time job.

Guidelines for Youthful Money Management

1. Assess your child's financial needs and wants. Supply their needs, but provide less than they want—significantly less.

2. Allow youngsters to experience the consequences of their management skills.

3. Include children (when it's appropriate) in family financial planning.

4. Never make the allowance conditional upon chores and household responsibilities.

176

5. Once the allowance is initiated, don't monitor what the children spend.

A Final Note

Remember, allowances are primarily tools for education and encouragement. You'll reap the benefits when kids begin to assume responsibility for their wardrobes, party gifts, and impulse items.

Try to balance children's needs with *your* responsibilities; their wants with *their* responsibilities, and nurture autonomy without undermining security.

PART FOUR
PARENTS AS PEOPLE

16
ALLY IN THE HOUSE:
Balancing The Partnership

A world where there are no parents, only assembly lines of fertility machines is a chilling one. But an even more frightening prospect is a world in which only psychologists would train and license those few parents declared psychologically fit to raise our children.

—Jeane Westin
The Coming Parent Revolution

NO MARRIAGE IS AN ISLAND

Your marriage began as a commitment between the two of you and if you're lucky it will end that way as well. Unfortunately, as families grow and children get older, marriages can be badly strained. There is more than a coincidental relationship between the onset of adolescence and divorce. If your marriage is to survive as the children mature, your marriage must mature as well. There is no admonition intended here. I'm not prescribing marriage at all costs—sacrificing everything for the kids including yourself. In a few short years the kids will be gone and your marital relationship will be reduced to its basic elements again—the two of you. Therefore, you're entitled to invest yourself in your marriage for its own sake; you're entitled to happiness and intimacy.

In addition, the relationship you have with your spouse, regardless of its quality or style, will have a profound impact on your children. As Adler noted, the first cooperation among other people which children see is the cooperation (or lack of it) in their parents' marriage.

Further, there seems to be a strong correlation between cooperation exhibited by spouses and the effectiveness of their child-rearing strategies. If both parents are in agreement about parenting issues, their child-rearing practices seem to be more effective and readily accepted by children.

To summarize, there are three critical and perhaps obvious reasons to foster intimacy and cooperation in your marriage: 1) to insure the survival of the marriage for your own sake; 2) to demonstrate effective cooperation for the children's benefit; and 3) to strengthen the only alliance you will have in the parenting process.

To insure your marriage survives and to provide a healthy model of cooperation for your children, it will be important to understand how your own emotional style affects your marriage and parenting practices. The behavior of your children is often a barometer of your marital relationship. In fact, several practitioners suggest that disturbing children are just symptom carriers of disturbed marriages. While this isn't always the case, the point is that no one is neutral in interpersonal interactions; everyone's actions are purposeful and goal-directed; and your marriage has provided the medium in which your children pursued their goals and found their place.

In other words, the emotional style of your marriage provides the field upon which your children will practice using their emotions and behavior. As a consequence, when things are chaotic in your marriage, your kids are often the same way. To understand and cope with the behavior of your kids, it's often necessary to focus your attentions on your marriage first.

ONE PLUS ONE = MORE THAN TWO

What initially attracted you to your mate during the early days of your relationship? Which things were most important to you? If you're like most people, you'll say that, in part, the attraction was based upon attributes possessed by the person that fulfilled needs you had. You'll probably also note your own ability to meet the needs of the other person. These two things, dependencies and strengths, established the style of intimacy in your relationship, and eventually, in your family.

In order to establish intimacy, (emotional, physical and spiritual closeness) it's imperative to understand the role your own emotional style plays. People seek to fulfill their own inadequacies and adequacies through their mates. Therefore, your statement of what attracted you to your mate reveals more about you than it does about your partner.

For example, you might have been attracted to your mate initially because you saw him/her as sensitive, a good listener, and perhaps, decisive. While you saw your partner as sensitive and decisive, you may have been searching for someone to balance your indecisiveness in an understanding (sensitive) way. Ideally, the inadequacies and strengths of you and your spouse ought to be balanced, but most of us are a little out of balance from time to time.

These assets and liabilities are unique for each of us, but some generalizations can be made regarding emotional styles. Some psychologists call these emotional styles "psychological priorities." These priorities define or describe our emotional styles because they establish our emotional goals as well as our emotional Achilles' heels—those emotions we most want to avoid. And, these priorities play a major role in defining our marriage and family life. In order to build and maintain marital intimacy, it's helpful to understand your own priorities.

PSYCHOLOGICAL PRIORITIES

According to psychologist Nira Kefir, there are four priorities or emotional styles which can be used as general descriptions for each of our personalities (but within these each of us will find our unique differences). The four general psychological priorities or styles suggested by Kefir include: pleasing, superiority-seeking, controlling, and avoiding. Your marriage joined two of these styles, so now the question is, What are yours? How do you identify them? More importantly, how do priorities affect your marriage and your parent-child relationships?

Identifying Your Priorities

For a moment fantasize that having read this book you are hereby entitled to the coupon of a lifetime. The coupon entitles you to exactly what it implies, a gift of a lifetime. Whatever your fondest desire, it will be provided—eternal happiness, one million dollars, political power, or your favorite sexual fantasy.

There's always a hitch, though. Along with the coupon go four qualifying conditions you must meet in order to get the gift. As you read these conditions below, rank order them from 1 to 4, based upon how difficult you would find them to do. That is, number one would be the most difficult and offensive, two the second most offensive, and four would be the least difficult or easiest for you to do. The four conditions are: 1) to make several (more than 5) sexual advances toward a loved one and be rejected on each occasion; 2) to work the remainder of your career in a commune where everyone is equal in status; competition and awards are not allowed; 3) to be shot in the shoulder with a gun (non-fatal, caliber of your choice); and 4) to go to a party with your spouse and have your secret lover show up; the lover is neither bright nor discreet.

Now rank these in order from the hardest to the easiest: 1, 2, 3, 4. Having made your selections you have identified those emotional situations which cause you the greatest stress—your own Achilles' heel. By examining those things you most hope to avoid you have also identified, below your awareness, those emotional situations which you desire most. These two things in combination—what you desire most and what you hope to avoid most—define your psychological priority.

You and your partner each have a strong orientation toward one of these priorities. In brief, the marriage of two people brings together two psychological styles which form a relationship, or what might be called a "relationship style." Given Kefir's four styles, there are ten possible marital combinations: control-control, please-superior, please-control, etc. Each of these combinations establishes a unique marital relationship and family atmosphere. Discussing all ten combinations at this point goes beyond the scope of this book. But, although the explanation here is very simplistic, understanding your own priority is instructive and potentially encouraging for your marriage and subsequently your children.

1. Pleasing Partners as Parents

If you selected number one—the pleasing priority—you abhor rejection. Conversely, you may try to be accepted by meeting the expectations of others—you "cain't say no." You are easily persuaded and depend heavily upon approval of others for self-esteem. You're obliging, charming, and pleasant to be with. These attributes are tremendous assets when first impressions are important. When you meet stress, when you become threatened by rejection, you may attempt to insure your belonging with others by showering them with service.

Pleasing others, then, often becomes equated with providing service. Service and love become synonymous, and the scales of service must always be in balance. If you (or your partner) have a pleasing style, your need to be accepted may be prepotent to the child's need for a parental leader. If both partners can't say no, the child may be placed in the awkward position of having to be the decision-maker.

Saying No without Being Rejected

The positive impact of pleasing parental styles is that children observe and enjoy the relaxed, spontaneous atmosphere in the marriage. But kids may take advantage of the relaxed atmosphere by being emotionally demanding or sulky, and by threatening rejection or withdrawing love.

So, you might ask, "How do I say no without losing my charm or being rejected?" Surprisingly, you can do this by watching yourself continue your present behavior. A simple one-week exercise can help. Respond to all of the requests and demands made of you by your partner and kids for a week. Record the emotional payoffs reaped and the prices paid. Then take note: are your payoffs worth the price you paid? In all probability they're not.

Having weighed the emotional price you pay against the payoffs you get when you refuse to say "no," ask your mate to list two things s/he always asks you to do that s/he could and should be doing. During the next week, if your mate asks you to do either one of these things, say no. Then assess the impact this benign strategy has on your parenting behavior. Your kids will notice the difference and what children see is what they'll believe.

2. Superior Partners as Parents

If you selected number two—that working in a commune was the most difficult for you—you may have a strong need to be superior to

185

others, to be one-up and you may spend inordinate amounts of time ranking yourself and everyone else. In an effort to be right, better, and smarter, you may form alliances with your children in order to defeat your mate. These alliances are always disruptive to the marriage and family. If alliances between children and parents become stronger than the alliances between partners, useless behaviors may develop in the child because the child's loyalties are strained.

Similarly, parents who try to maintain supremacy by being the star or superior person usually use their children as a means of seeking excellence as well. They demand to be recognized as superior parents and professionals, often holding their children accountable to higher standards than they hold themselves. These aspirations are very burdensome for children. High expectations can have a paradoxical effect on extremely ambitious parents. In these cases, Kahlil Gibran's poem rings loudly in our ears, "Seek not to live through your children." They can never be what we ourselves wanted to be and couldn't.

You can raise your consciousness concerning your need for superiority by observing your emotions and behavior in regard to two things: competitiveness and intolerance. For a week privately chart your reactions to your mate concerning these two emotions. Do you feel compelled to correct or surpass your partner financially and intellectually? Are you intolerant of your partner's tardiness, ambition, or social appearance? Give your spouse permission to count the number of times you employ superiority inappropriately during the week. Based upon the outcome, assess the impact of these attributes on your marriage and the children.

Now try eliminating one of these transactions with your mate each week. Observe the impact this has on parenting. Your kids will decide how committed you are to equality based on how much of it they see in your marriage. Probably, while focusing on your marriage, you have improved your adult-child relationships as well.

3. Avoiding Partners as Parents

If you chose number three you're probably very sensitive to pain—emotional as well as physical. If you thought being shot was the most distasteful, you cannot bear to experience any discomfort or insecurity. You may spend your energies avoiding anything that threatens security.

186

You're not unpleasant to be with; you're compassionate and sensitive to the needs of others. But the same compassion that makes you nurturing as a parent can also make you hypersensitive in the eyes of others.

Your hypersensitivity may put your mate in the position of walking on eggshells. Children may sense that there is unfinished business in your marriage. Thus, the kids of avoiding parents often serve as conflict detours for their parents. For example, when Mom and Dad are about to have conflict the kids will create a crisis which will dwarf Mom and Dad's problems. Every time the marital relationship approaches conflict, children feel compelled unconsciously to rescue their parents from marital disaster by focusing their attention on useless behavior. In these cases the children's useless behaviors serve as a distracting side show. Parents must attend to the useless goals and are temporarily prevented from having, or resolving, their marital difficulties. Thus, in a case like this one, the effect your sensitivity has on the marital relationship is one thing, and the effect it has on the children in the family is quite another.

Avoiding Stress without Pain

If you are an avoider, entertain your wildest aversion and take it to its illogical end; in other words, dream up the worst case you can for the dreaded "what if..." Once the catastrophe is vividly in mind, write it down and read it aloud to yourself and your spouse. Then, post these around the house for family members to see. Some examples might include: "I will never move again and want to be buried in the back yard." "You must never die on me." "I intend to parade through your office unannounced with three babies in diapers on a regular basis, to discourage your colleagues from having the affair with you that I know they want." Once these ideas are out in the open, their absurdity has a funny way of defusing your anxiety.

Once your children realize that you are no longer intimidated by stress, that you feel secure and are willing to endure a little discomfort, they won't try to rescue or intimidate you nearly as much.

4. Controlling Partners as Parents

If you chose number four, you probably felt it would be physically impossible to go to the party because of the public exposure and humiliation it might bring: thus you will identify with the controlling personality. You might feel like a social philodendron at times, like a social plant. It isn't passivity, but an active aversion to social interaction; an aversion to the potential for embarrassment and humiliation, and loss of emotional control. Your emotional control makes you dependent upon routine, schedules, and organization in order to avoid public embarrassment. A true nightmare for you is a surprise party. Of course, there is good news about this style as well. Your spouse and kids see you as dependable, stable, and conscientious.

Giving Up Control without Losing It

You may try to soften your controlling style with your kids, but if you continue to manipulate your mate with stoicism and rules, your children may try to liberate your mate. Sensing that one parent is handcuffed by the other, children may try to add power to one end of the equation in order to balance things. So, it isn't ususual to see children of controlling partners become the reverse puppets described in an earlier chapter. The private logic of these children expesses their belief that "You may boss my Mom/Dad, but you can't boss me!"

Therefore, you should not only be more democratic with your kids, but seek equality in your marriage as well. Ask each family member, beginning with your spouse, to make a short list of three things in their lives that you routinely try to control that are annoying to them. Then, monitor your behavior for a week. At the end of the week make a list of emotional prices you paid for attempting to control as well as the payoffs provided. Whose behavior is most predictable—yours or others'? What impact did your behavior have on your marriage and what impact did your behavior have on the children? Each family member will have a unique reaction to covert or overt dominance of one parent over the other. Inevitably, when one parent feels controlled or dominated, the ripples of revolution will include one or more of the children.

During the coming week, invite your family to tell you when your need to be boss interferes with them. Agree upon a signal or device to avoid conflict. For example, when Dad is overly involved in Sue's after-school friends, Sue can say, "I can handle it, Dad." Or, "I'm not bothering you am I, Dad?" These exchanges might help clarify how much "stuff" you take on that doesn't belong to you.

These techniques are not panaceas for every relationship, but they can provide an opportunity to negotiate rather than dictate. It is always advisable to seek professional help if these ideas aren't working for you. If you are locked desperately in your own set of needs, a professional may be needed to help break the deadlock.

RENEGOTIATING INTIMACY

If your marriage is to survive, you'll have to cooperate with your mate, and in the process your children will see (and believe in) how it's done. You'll have to stop the useless dance of your priorities around the trivial as well as essential tasks of life in order to try to insure intimacy (emotional, physical, and spiritual closeness).

Alienation of affection is most often created by the way you handle the ongoing and everyday aspects of life, not the dramatic or catastrophic. Research evidence suggests in fact, that among first marriages, chores, money, parenting, and sex are the culprits of devastation, in that order. Among second and third marriages the list has a different order: 1) parenting; 2) money; 3) chores; and 4) sex.

Although couples have sexual concerns at times and there often are legitimate dysfunctions, most sexual problems are political problems that develop in the other life tasks and migrate into the bedroom as political dirty tricks. Intimacy is devastated by the mundane, not by sexual fixations. Freud assumed that because his clients had sexual dysfunctions, all of their problems were sexual. It's a dramatic example of finding what you're looking for.

When couples slide into despair, sex is often the last thing to deteriorate. The reverse can also be true. Yet, if we relied upon sexual problems to account for every fractured relationship, we would be left with no corrective actions because many couples continue to copulate madly, but don't cooperate past the edge of the bed! The irony, of course, is that although marital disintegration is brought on by the mundane and trivial, frequently it only reaches our consciousness when sexual dissatisfaction or infidelity forces us to shift our attention to the other issues.

Rearing children, holding them accountable for their chores, and managing a household of four or more people can easily transform a loving, sexy ally into a repulsive adversary. Renegotiating and rekindling intimate relationships, which are constantly bombarded indiscriminately by six- and sixteen-year-olds requires creativity. For some couples, intimacy—sexual and otherwise—is so rare that their only memory of it is having talked in the bathroom while one shaved and the other bathed. Occasionally, after encouraging a couple to talk about sexual intimacy, I discover they both think orgasm is the name of a punk rock group—that's trouble! If you can remember what initially attracted you to your mate, there is hope. A little guided fantasy can help develop or rekindle strategies for intimacy. Remember when...

REMEMBER WHEN...?

Remember the luxurious Saturday mornings sleeping until 9:15 and caressing each other awake? Now luxury is waking at 7:30 A.M. to the blare of Saturday cartoons and having only two kids in bed with you. Remember retiring at a sexy hour (11:30), reading, bathing, and building each other to a slow candelight crescendo? Now you crumble into bed at midnight, hoping to lapse into a coma before your partner does, so s/he will be stirred awake by the youngest child's ritual nightmare at 2:00 A.M.

Remember those cool, fall Sunday afternoons in front of the fire, falling asleep watching the Giants squeak by Atlanta 33-7 and waking in each other's arms with the afternoon sun high upon the family room wall? Now, Sunday afternoons are considered blissful if less than half a dozen neighborhood children tour your bedroom playing "Century Twenty-One." You consider it an extra bonus if "60 Minutes" rolls around without any lacerations, broken bones, or fevers serious enough to warrant a visit to the emergency room. And, the weekend is an intimate success if drop-in guests are limited to one wave of shirt-tail relatives who leave Sunday night, and you're lucky enough to sleep on the mattress pad of your own bed.

Making Intimacy

Make intimacy? "Sure...before kids!" you say? Of course, kids absorb some of the time we used to devote to one another, but not all of it.

It's more likely that another scenario unfolded. Let's say, as an example, that your need for superiority wasn't totally quenched through your spouse's affirmation of your greatness. So, you turned to career, the accomplishments of the kids, and success on the school board in order to acquire a sense of greatness. As the other things provided new sources of affirmation, you slowly turned away from that most basic source of sustenance—your mate. Now is the time to turn back.

You can't bring back the good old days, but you can renegotiate the intimacy your relationship requires. To make sure that you and your partner are parenting allies and bedroom lovers, you may have to talk and act differently. By using the assets while minimizing the liabilities of your psychological priorities as described earlier, you and your partner can initiate more cooperation in your marriage. Intimacy, cooperation, and respect are won, not bought, through a commitment to equality by both partners. Your children will develop their own emotional style based on the way you treat them. However, ultimately, their style will be based upon how you and your partner treat one another.

17

SUPERMOM/DAD:
Perils of the Single Parent

Life is only softly determined.

—F.M.

LEAPING ONE PROBLEM AT A TIME

Two teachers sit in the teachers' lounge grading papers. Casually one turns to the other and says, "You had Tom last year, didn't you? He's a problem, isn't he! But you know, his Mom/Dad is raising him alone!" This comment raises the hobgoblin that Tom's misconduct is generated by some moral failing of the single parent! In addition, a mental image is conjured up of dirty-faced children running wild while Mom is at work in the garment factory. Not true—or at least no truer for the single- than for the two-parent family. The stereotype of the "broken home" is just that—a stereotype. One five-year-old, hearing her home described as "broken," declared, "Our home isn't broken—it works!" Exactly. A single-parent home works as well or better than many homes where the couples remain embattled; the single-parent family can work as well as any family if everyone encourages each other.

Contrary to another popular idea, "single parent" is not synonymous with being a swinging single. Far from it. In fact, if you fought for custody of the children—and can still remember why—you should file for endangered species status; you're rare.

However, single parents are as guilty of being biased by those stereotypes as anyone. In fact, if you are parenting alone, your need to refute these myths may drive you even harder than other people toward the perfect parent fiction. The unconscious pressure to be like "normal" families can evoke a compensatory attitude of "I must do it all."

SUPER PARENT

Parents who are raising their children with a partner have the luxury of the illusion that the kids' shabby behavior is their mate's fault. If you're a single parent, there's no excuse—or so it seems. Every aspect of the child's life comes to rest at your door.

Kids going to school in less than perfectly coordinated Geranimals raise eyebrows: "S/he's working you know; doesn't have time to dress them properly." Gossip like this, whether real or imagined, leads single parents into a unique kind of double bind. Thinking that the children are shortchanged by having only one parent in the home, the single parent tries to do double duty in a thinly veiled attempt to be Supermom or Superdad. Aside from the fact that striving for such perfection is useless for the child, it's destructive for the parent.

Chris, mother of two young sons, provides an example. "Every night, no matter how tired I was, I went through the bedtime ritual with the boys—brushed their teeth, read them a story, heard their prayers. Each night I felt that I couldn't go through this routine one more time, but what would happen to the kids if I didn't?"

What happened was this: Chris's sister, a married mother of sons, visited late one night and nonchalantly commented, "Are you still tucking the boys in?"

"Yes," said Chris. "Don't you?"

"Sometimes I do. Sometimes they go to bed by themselves."

Chris laughed out loud. "You mean I don't *have* to tuck them in?"

"Why would you think you have to?" asked the incredulous sister.

The answer to that question reveals two important points for single parents. First, all too often, single parents believe they *have* to do everything for and with their children or in some way, albeit obscure and difficult to define, the children will suffer. Second, for singles there is no spouse to question these beliefs, to mull over what should and shouldn't be done, to give permission not to be perfectly on duty at all times.

Another pitfall of single parenting is living one's life through the children. Initially you may build your schedules around the children for logistical purposes. Then, without realizing it, the children's social schedules become your social life as well. While your children can create new experiences for you, if you become dependent on them, you are prone to discouragement and unhealthy loyalties.

For Moms and Dads going it alone, both of the difficulties discussed above—the lack of objectivity and the limited social life—can be relieved tremendously by single-parent support groups. To locate such a group, try a church, community center, or telephone book. A good support network is a vital help to restore and maintain equilibrium in one's life.

SPECIAL PROBLEMS FOR THE SINGLE PARENT

While single Moms and Dads can be as encouraged and encouraging as married mothers and fathers, still there are some life tasks which require special attention and extra energy for singles. The next few pages offer a brief look at just a few of these challenges.

Visitation

When divorce is the cause for single parenting, visitation is undoubtedly the anxiety-producing issue. Even in the face of court orders, two people can distort rulings beyond recognition. Typically, one or both parents use visitation as a means of muscling the other.

The parent with custody often assumes a position as guard of the visitation schedule. At times this can be a very powerful position, but it also becomes a heavy responsibility. Children can easily become pawns in a parental power struggle or the reverse can occur: children pit one parent against the other.

To diffuse these struggles, one parent should not voluntarily assume or demand to determine the scheduling of all visits. Instead, as soon as children are able to voice a reasoned opinion about their schedules, visitation should be negotiated democratically and cooperatively with all parties. This can be accomplished via conference calls and prearranged negotiation meetings. Unilateral control of visitation is certain to create ongoing combat among parents and children.

Space

There are certain things that cause anxiety, although they are supposed to be routine. One of these is space, not the currently popular definition of psychological "space," but actual physical space—as in "My bedroom is ten feet from your playroom" or "Your bedroom is not my bedroom," and so forth. The physical accommodations of the newly single parent may be cramped and always *feel* different, even if the abode is the same. While there may be very little you can do about this, do everything you can. Tight space may require scheduling rooms, buying sliding doors and even installing locks. While these gestures are more symbolic than substantive, parents and kids must be able to put physical distance between themselves in a voluntary way.

Special Time

Single parents are inclined to believe they spend too much time with their kids or don't have the energy for them after doing everything else required in a day. The strategy of "special time" can be especially effective here. Remember there is a definite difference between being at home with your child and spending quality or special time with him or her.

Children of single parents are trying to fill a void, just as the parent is. To secure a place with you, the child may demand exclusive access to you. S/he may monopolize all relationships with adults. As a result, the most casual of visits may be disrupted by attention-getting mechanisms which would otherwise not be used.

By scheduling time with children, it's possible to demonstrate to them that their place with you is guaranteed. When single parents take time to schedule special time arrangements, they actually have more freedom. Once children feel secure, children's irrational demands for attention will subside and then disappear.

Love and Intimacy

Defining yourself in terms of the man or woman in your life is discouraging business. Yet, love and intimacy are as essential to the human condition as oxygen. No matter why you are parenting alone, at some point you need intimacy. But your chances of gaining closeness may be dead if you don't attend to the task. If you unconsciously prepare a romantic meal and then remember you're eating with a five-year-old, or if the sexiest movie you can remember seeing is "Star Wars," you're probably not taking care of yourself. Two brief rules of thumb for this situation are 1) don't compensate for feeling neglectful by being self-sacrificing, and 2) don't rush into any relationship because you think it might be better for the kids.

When another person enters a parent's life, children usually react strongly, regardless of the person's inherent goodness. Reason and fairness don't taint children's perceptions. Children think that a stranger—who neither represents nor holds a candle to their true parent—is trying to replace the biological parent. Although children's resentment is generated indiscriminately, it's important to understand their sense of abandonment and jealousy. They feel as if the new person in their lives is taking their parent away.

Reacting to this perceived emotional robbery, children outdo themselves trying to sabotage the new relationship. For example, illness may strike at the most inopportune moment—perhaps just as you and your friend are about to leave for an important date. If you are starting a new relationship, this could induce enough guilt for you to cancel the evening and stay home. Another quick guideline is this: don't abandon your children, but do make provision for these unexpected events and continue with your plans.

Feelings of rejection and rebellion usually go hand-in-hand. When children feel displaced or dethroned by a new adult, they experience it as rejection. Following a divorce, children internalize their rejection so intensely that they temporarily seek the useless goal of revenge. You may not see the logic in this, but the kids do. War is declared based on this sense of rejection, and battlefields erupt at the least expected and least desirable times.

The best strategy for new relationships is to talk openly with the new person and your kids about the issues and emotions at stake. Utilize the communication skills outlined previously for problem-solving: 1) voice observations and avoid judgment and blame; 2) maintain eye contact and attend to the youngster or mate; 3) reflect what others have said; 4) work at reflecting content and emotion; and 5) use "I" statements, taking responsibility for your own emotions and behavior. For example, rather than indicting the child by accusing, "You're always so mean when s/he comes to call," an "I" statement may help. "I am really hurt when..."

Finally, love and intimacy can be destroyed by your own attitude alone. Early apprehensions which have gone unresolved can cause disaster. You may use the children as an excuse to avoid closeness. More than one courtship has been toppled by the self-defeating belief that "the children won't understand and won't be able to handle it," or "it isn't fair to the children." However, simply because children *feel* rejected does not mean that they *are* being rejected. Therefore, don't project or amplify your own emotions onto your kids.

Work

So you're now the breadwinner and the sole person responsible for the financial well-being of the children until they're eighteen. This is a sobering prospect. On the lighter side, work can be an encouraging aspect of life. It may mean a new career, challenges, and self-esteem. However, when work provides only money, it becomes "toil," a distinction described by Mortimer Adler, and, as such, has the potential to degrade our existence and strip us of our humanity.

Parenting alone has the potential to make work "toil." If you have ever ushered your last appointment of the day into your office at 4:30 P.M. and that person has to step over your four-year-old napping on the floor, you understand how complicated work can be. Employers and clients usually aren't very sympathetic to your logistical problems. Convincing your boss to let you take your morning break before work so you can deliver your son to nursery school isn't easy. Getting a lunch break at 1:30 in order to get a daughter to the dentist isn't much better. Perhaps the worst is the panic that sweeps your body when you remember, in the middle of a 7:00 business dinner, that you forgot to pick up your children at 6:00!

Children will have to make sacrifices to support your occupation so you will be able to support them. Being "latch-key" kids doesn't mean children have to be irresponsible and unsupervised. Reasonable rules should be set in advance, like not allowing neighborhood children into the home until you or a sitter is there. Most children actually enjoy the autonomy of going home after school, fixing a PBJ, and having the house to themselves for an hour or two.

As a single parent, you can consider the children's time alone an opportunity—an opportunity to generate meaningful responsibilities like the good ol' days. In the morning the kids have a chance to get up without nagging, prepare their own lunches, and remember their own wraps. All this builds a sense of accomplishment and competence and doesn't have to make you feel neglectful. It's helpful to remember that many children from two-parent homes are asked to assume these responsibilities as well.

Finally, the single parent has the opportunity to make his or her children career-conscious. When children are forced to adjust to the flow of the parent's career, they become career-conscious at an early age. Be optimistic; use these awarenesses to enhance the children's sense that "they can handle it."

Single Parent Special Time

It doesn't take long to recognize that single parents are not only entitled to, but desperately need their own special time. Whatever the activity chosen, the time spent is not important—it's critical, whether it's a day at the lake, a night on the town, or a weekend at home while the kids are at Grandma's.

Why is this necessary? As a brief example, single parents are like deep-sea divers who have been submerged for extended periods of time. Like the diver at home in the water, the single parent is at home in the world inside the family, but as he or she surfaces, s/he feels the pain of transition. These social "bends" are earnest detriments to health. Special time for single parents is the decompression chamber for the social bends.

A final word to Superdads and Supermoms—if you live your life as if nothing is required or desired beyond your parental responsibilities, you are *actively* holding the world at bay. Life without intimacy may be "simpler" in some ways, but in the long run, it's discouraging—both for you and the children. Take steps to bring balance to your life. Go forward with confidence knowing that just like your children, you can handle it.

In truth, the principles offered here are applicable to all parents, single or otherwise. Single parents have all the predicaments and responsibilities that couples do in addition to special circumstances. In a sense, they have half the time to devote to the task and twice as much responsibility. This chapter doesn't presume to address, let alone solve, all the special concerns and struggles of the single parent; only to suggest the *principles* offered here are equally applicable to their circumstances.

18
"YEAH, BUT..."

*The pleasure of being a parent isn't reasonable
or objective...It is the extraordinary experience
of having short people who hang around awhile,
who change you as they change, who push and
prod and aggravate and thrill you and make life
fuller. Who are, more than anything else, irra-
tionally special to you.*

—*Ellen Goodman*
Close to Home

YEAH...

Having come this far, you may still have trouble taking action on the
suggestions made. That's okay. That means you recognize and understand what it is that needs to be done, but you're having a hard time
bringing yourself to do it. The "yeah" of recognition acknowledges
that the strategies that have been proposed are reasonable; the "but,"
includes a residue of reticence.

FIX' EM

As parents, we usually think in terms of "fix' em," meaning the kids, when looking to change our families. We expect something somehow to change the child's behavior. As time passes, we realize the fix will have to include "em" and "us." The hesitant "Yeah" reflects recalcitrant ownership of fix *us* as well as fix *'em*. Solutions can't be accomplished without expenditure of calories and hard work. But in the long run, parenting becomes easier, more gratifying and enjoyable. However, parenting will never be effortless or painless.

THE SHABBY "BUT"

The "but" in "yeah, but" comes from knowing what you should do, but being privately committed to the old ways. The "but" discloses your reluctance to forfeit fictitious control. And, it might punctuate the extent to which you find your own place by needing to be needed. The achiever, outdoer, and pleaser may all have some difficulty utilizing logical consequences, but each for his/her own reason. Whatever the reason, try giving up the old ways.

YOU CAN HANDLE IT!

In the final analysis, congruent with the system suggested in the preceding chapters, the choice is yours. Ask yourself at what risk change is made and to what end. Are your current parenting practices helping to rear a responsible eighteen-year-old? The items below are a final test of your readiness for change.

1. If you still feel your self-worth is dependent upon your three-year-old's bowel movements, it may be unwise to give up feces fights. On the other hand, if you have determined that his/her sphincter is out of your control, you're ready to move.

2. If you are still letting a bundt cake do your talking and "Oh Yuk," threatens your parenthood and sensuality, you're not ready. But if you believe in pursuing your esteem through your own efforts you're ready for the Black and Decker award for handling power tools.

3. When your seven-year-old meets you at the store dressed like a clown and you run to the next aisle to avoid embarrassment,

don't rush to begin these techniques. But, when you can act as if he is a casual acquaintance and not yours, you're ready to wear a "The kid dressed himself" pin.

4. If you are impressed by suffering—yours or your kids'—don't give up the "Grimmys." But if suffering seems sordid and tacky, you're ready to give up martyrdom or being controlled by it.

5. Finally, if you have heart palpitations when you think about your kids leaving home and the oldest is six, you're not ready to implement the strategies offered in this book. But if you have sexual fantasies about the good old days, you're a candidate to succeed with these strategies no matter how old your kids are.

What is offered here is courage through humor, support through pragmatic techniques, hope through demonstrated success, understanding through personal experience, self-acceptance via ownership of imperfection, and optimism through a commitment to encouragement. You aren't perfect, but now—"you can handle it."

BIBLIOGRAPHY

Adler, A. *Science of Living*. New York: Doubleday and Co., 1964.

Adler, A. *What Life Should Mean to You*. New York: Capricorn Books, 1958.

Allred, Hugh. *How to Strengthen Your Marriage and Family*. Salt Lake City: Brigham House, 1976.

Ansbacher, H.L. & Ansbacher, R.R., eds. *The Individual Psychology of Alfred Adler*. New York: Basic Books, Inc., 1956, paper.

Bader, E., Microys, G., Sinclair, C., Willet, E. & Conway, B. "Do Marriage Preparation Programs Really Work? A Canadian Experiment." *Journal of Marital and Family Therapy*, April, 1980, Vol. 6, No. 2, 171-180.

Beecher, Marguerite & Beecher, William. *Beyond Success and Failure: Ways of Self-reliance and Maturity*. New York: Julian Press, 1966.

Bly, Carol. *Letters from the Country*. New York: Harper & Row, 1981.

Browne, J. *The Comparison of Two Methods of Identifying Personality Priorities*. Maryland: B.F. Associates, 1977.

Browning, Elizabeth Barrett. *Sonnets from the Portuguese*. Edited by William Peterson. New York: Barre Publishing, 1977.

Christensen, O. & Thomas, C. "A Model for Counseling: The Significant Entourage in the Treatment of Depression." *The Individual Psychologist*, 1978, Vol. 15, No. 3, 15-24.

Clark, I.C. *Elizabeth Barrett Browning*. Port Washington, N.Y.: Kennikat Press. Reissued 1970, first 1929.

Corsini, Raymond & Ignas, Edward. *Alternative Educational Systems*. Itasca, Illinois: F.E. Peacock Publishers, Inc., 1982.

Del Vecchio, John. *The 13th Valley*. New York: Bantam Books, Inc., 1983.

Dinkmeyer, D. & Pew, W.L. *Adlerian Counseling and Psychotherapy*. Monterey, California: Brooks/Cole Publishing Co., 1979.

Dreikurs, R. *Coping with Children's Misbehavior*. New York: Hawthorn Press, 1972.

Dreikurs, R. *Discipline without Tears*. Toronto: Alfred Adler Institute, 1972.

Dreikurs, R. *Maintaining Sanity in the Classroom*. New York: Harper & Row, 1971.

Dreikurs, R. *Psychodynamics, Psychotherapy, and Counseling: Collected Papers*. Chicago: Alfred Adler Institute, 1967.

Dreikurs, R. *Psychology in the Classroom*. New York: Harper & Row, 1968.

Dreikurs, R. & Soltz, V. *Children: The Challenge*. New York: Duell, Sloan & Pearce, 1964.

Elder, Glen. *Children of the Great Depression: Social Change in Life Experience*. Chicago: University of Chicago Press, 1974.

Fromm, E. *The Anatomy of Human Destructiveness*. New York: Holt, Rinehart & Winston, 1973.

Gibran, K. *The Prophet*. New York: Knopf, 1923.

Gordon, T. *P.E.T. in Action*. New York: Wyden Books, 1976.

Keillor, Garrison. *Happy to Be Here: Stories and Comic Pieces*. New York: Atheneum Books, 1982.

Kelly, J. & Main, F. "Sibling Conflict in a Single Parent Family: An Empirical Case Study." *American Journal of Family Therapy*, Spring, 1979, Vol. 7, No. 1.

Langenfeld, S. & Main, F. "Personality Priorities: A Factor Analytic Study of Individual Psychology." *Journal of Adlerian Psychology: Journal of Research Theory and Practice*, March, 1983, Vol. 39, No.1.

Lewis, C.R. "Elizabeth Barrett Browning's Family Disease: Anorexia." *American Journal of Family Therapy*, January, 1982, Vol. 8, No. 1, 124-142.

Minuchin, S. *Families and Family Therapy*. Cambridge, Mass.: Harvard University Press, 1974.

Minuchin, S. *Psychosomatic Families: Anorexia Nervosa in Context*. Cambridge, Mass,: Harvard University Press, 1978.

Mosak, H. *On Purpose: Collected Papers*. Chicago: Alfred Adler Institute, 1977.

O'Connell, W. & Bright, M. *Natural High Primer*. Veterans Hospital Houston, Texas, 1977.

Shulman, B. *Essays in Schizophrenia*. Baltimore: Williams & Wilkins, 1968.

Spock, Benjamin, M.D. *Raising Children in a Difficult Time*. New York: W.W. Norton & Co., Inc., 1974.

Walsh, T. "Endocrine Disturbances in Anorexia Nervosa and Depression." *Psychosomatic Medicine*, March, 1982, Vol. 44, No. 1.

Yager, J. "Family Issues in Pathogenesis of Anorexia." *Psychosomatic Medicine*, March, 1982, Vol. 44, No. 1.

INDEX

Encouraging parenting, 8, 52-53, 57-76, 167.
Equality, 93. *See also* Family council.
Extortion, 171.
Extremism, 7.

F.A.C.E.N., 89.
Fairness, 9-10.
Family car. *See* Driving.
Family as social model, 3-4. *See also* Family council.
Family benefits, 58-59.
Family council, 99-108.
Family heirarchy. *See* Birth order.
Family survival, 6.
Fear, 122.
Fighting, 147-153. *See also* Table squabbles.
Financial responsibility, 172-176.
First born, 31-34.
Forgetfulness, 128-130.
Freedom, 5.

Getting even. *See* Revenge.
Gibran, Kahil, 112, 184.
Givum reflex, 172.
Good behavior. *See* Buying good behavior.
Groins and armpits, 4-5.

Healthy personality development, 58.
Hearing skills, 69-73. *See also* Being heard; Communication.
Hopelessness, 28.
Hugging, 12-13.
Humor, 61.
Hunger strikes, 12. *See also* Anorexia; Eating problems.

Ice cream responses, 65-67. *See also* Communication; Hearing skills; Listening.
Imperfection, 2, 10. *See also* Perfection.
Independence, 6, 66.
Inflexibility, 33.
Injustice, 36, 38.
Intimacy, 179-189, 194-196.
Invitation-to-church trick, 160.
Irresponsibility. *See* Affluence and irresponsibility.

Kefir, Nira, 181.
Kelly and Main, 150.

Latch-key children, 196-197.
Lecturing your children, 63-65. *See also* Being heard.
Lewis, Carol, 164.
Liberal parenting, 7.
Listening, 61, 63-65.
skills, 68.
Logical consequences, 7, 9, 77, 81-82, 121, 134, 144, 146, 162. *See also* Alternative consequences; Natural consequences.

foundation for, 79.
guidelines for creating, 82.
Looming adults. *See* Groins and armpits.
Loyalties, children's, 184.

Mackenzie, Margaret, 2.
Management skills, 172-175.
Manipulating others, 32, 38-39, 43, 62, 65, 164, 167. *See also* Tyrannical children.
Marital intimacy, 10. *See also* Intimacy; Sexual dysfunction; Sexual intimacy.
Marriage partnership, 179-189.
Marriage priorities, 181-189.
Martyrdom, 163-169.
Mealtime problems. *See* Eating problems.
Media influence, 2.
Menu planning, 134-135, 140-142.
Me-sturbation, 3-4.
Middle child, 31-32, 34-37.
Misbehavior. See Attention-getting; Assumed disability; Emotional goals; Power; Revenge; Tantrums.
Montague, Ashley, 1-2.
Motivation, 29, 49, 59-60. *See also* Bribery.
Mystery box, 83-84.

Nagging, 83. *See also* Being heard.
Narcolepsy. *See* Oversleeping.
Natural consequences, 8, 80-81, 86, 105, 128-129, 140, 162. *See also* Alternative consequences; Logical consequences.
Nutrition, 135, 138.

Oldest child. *See* Firstborn.
Only child, 41-44.
Ovaries. See Power tools.
Oversleeping, 119-122. *See also* Sleep.
guidelines for, 121, 127-128.

Parental control, 2, 23, 163-164.
Parental guilt, 166.
Parenting styles, 6-7, 57, 180.
Pavlovian conditioning, 48, 59.
Perfect parent myth, 1-2, 63, 132, 134.
Perfection, 33, 44. *See also* Imperfection.
Perseverance, 34.
Pests. *See* Attention-getting mechanisms.
Pet praise, 50, 59-60, 62.
Pew, William, 166.
Phantom families, 1.
Policing children's fighting, 148-153.
Power, 12-13, 23-26, 122, 155, 165, 167, 172. *See also* Psychological power.
sharing, 99-100.
Power, bids for, 23-26, 85.
Power struggle, 23, 33, 65, 89, 96, 110-117, 120, 160, 165. *See also* Discipline.
Power tools (bowels, bladder, ovaries, testes and brain), 155-162.
guidelines for handling, 159-162.

Praise, 50.
Pregnancy. *See* adolescent sexuality.
Private logic, 16-19.
Psychological power, 155.
Psychological priorities, 181-187.
Punishment, 45, 47-51, 78, 83, 87, 162.
    alternatives to, 77.
    characteristics of, 79.
Punitive methods. *See* Punishment.

Rebellion, 25, 36, 109-117. *See also*
    Control; Discouragement; Emotional
    goals; Power, bids for; Reverse pup-
    pets; Tantrums; Useless behavior.
Reinforcement theory, 48.
Rejection, 12.
Rejection through food, 133-134, 182-
    183.
Reproduction, 159-162.
Reproductive organs. *See* Power tools.
Respect, 5, 52.
Responsibilities, children's, 5-6, 14-15,
    39-40, 52-53, 58, 60-62, 66, 107,
    119-132, 172, 175. *See also* Allow-
    ances; Chores; Family council; Menu
    planning; Teaching responsibility.
Revenge, 11-13, 26-28, 85-86, 165.
Reverse puppets, 109-111.
Reward strategy. *See* Bribery.
Rousseau, Jean Jacques, 7.
Running away, 165.

School phobia, 122-125, 127-128.
Secondborn child. *See* Middle child.
Seduction, 159-162.
Self-centeredness, 3-4.
Self-destructiveness, 28-29, 167. *See*
    also Assumed disability; Martyrdom.
Self-esteem, 4, 9, 39-40, 77, 107, 133-
    134, 183.
Self-sacrificing, 169.
Sexual dysfunction, 187-188.
Sexual intimacy, renegotiating, 187-189.
Sexuality. *See* Adolescent sexuality; Inti-
    macy.
Sibling table fights. *See* Table squabbles;
    Fighting.
Sibling warfare. *See* Fighting.
Single parenting, 191-198.
Sleep, 156-157.
Sleeping sickness. *See* Oversleeping.
Snacks, 135-136.
"Sonnets from the Portuguese," 164.
Sonstegard, Manford, 59.
Space and single parents, 194.
Special time, 93-97, 150, 194, 197-198.
    implementing, 94-96.
Spock, Dr. Benjamin, 7, 45.
Stress, avoiding, 185.
Success, opportunities for, 61.
Suffering. *See* Martyrdom.
Super parent, 192-193.
Supper hour. *See* Eating problems; Table
    squabbles.

Table squabbles, 142-143.
Tantrums, 16, 45-46, 50, 85, 110.
Teaching responsibility, 6.
Temper tantrums. *See* Tantrums.
Testes. *See* Power tools.
Threats, 47-48.
Time together, 61. *See also* Special time.
Toilet training, 157-159.
Training, time for, 61.
Trust child's abilities, 58-59, 64, 73-75,
    93, 158, 200.
Tyrannical children, 46, 49, 147-153.

Useful behavior, 19, 44.
Useless behavior, 15-16, 18, 22, 121,
    126, 166, 184.
Useless goals, 12, 60, 63, 165. *See also*
    Emotional goals.
    identifying, 84-85.

Visitation, 193.

Walsh, Dr. Timothy, 165.
Work and single parenting, 196-197.

Yager, Dr. Joel, 167.
Youngest child. *See* Baby of family.

ABOUT THE AUTHOR

Frank O. Main did his undergraduate work at Yankton College in Yankton, South Dakota. He received his M.A. from the University of Iowa, and his Ed.D. from Idaho State University. Currently, Dr. Main is associate professor of counseling at the University of South Dakota and director of the Family Education Center there. He is also a practicing clinical member of the American Association of Marriage and Family Therapy.

In addition to his academic and writing activities, Main conducts workshops in classroom behavior and family counseling, consults with educational institutions, and maintains a private practice in family therapy.

Frank and his wife Mary have two daughters, Katie and Buffie.